Writing Your First

WRITING YOUR FIRST NOVEL

Second Edition

John Reynolds

Starblaze Publications

Second edition published by Starblaze Publications

First published in 2006 by Polygraphia

Starblaze Publications
10A Law Street, Torbay, Auckland 0633, New Zealand
jbess@vodafone.co.nz

www.drjohnreynolds.com

A catalogue record for this book is available from the National Library of New Zealand.

Cover design by AnitaTaylorDesign.com

CONTENTS

1

THE DREAM

> If you would be a writer, write! —
> *Epictetus*

For many people the writing of a novel is a dream, something they'd love to do, something they've always wanted to do, or something they'll get round to doing one day – therefore, always only a dream.

Your dream can become a reality – if you're prepared to invest time and energy into realising it. The reality of holding a novel in your hands with your title and your name on the front cover – a dream come true.

Yes, there'll be plenty of people who will inform you that a novel is probably the most difficult type of book to have published, particularly if you're an unknown author or have no track record as a novelist; but don't let this put you off. There are ways and means.

This book is written primarily for the first time novel writer. Although I'm based in New Zealand I have travelled and worked in many other parts of the world and know that the advice and guidance I provide can apply to aspiring first time novel writers anywhere.

There are heaps of books and websites of varying quality providing you with information on many different types of writing, including the novel. However, if you've ever thought to yourself or even said to other people, "I'd love to write a novel," then this book will be of considerable interest and help to you.

As well as quoting from a variety of novels, I've deliberately chosen excerpts from my own first novel *Uncommon Enemy* as this enables me to directly share my first hand writing experiences with you – from the concept through to the final product. I have also included excerpts from my recently published young adult novel *Robyn Hood Outlaw Princess*. Both books are available as print or eBook on Amazon.com.

Motivation: The Essential Ingredient

Whether you're an experienced writer or regard yourself as a novice, the key ingredients are motivation, commitment and determination. Writing your novel will be a long process, spread over many months or even years. Yet if you really feel that you have a story to tell you'll do it. Yes, there will be challenges and setbacks, but at the same time your motivation will provide you with some wonderful moments as you watch your story take shape and bring your characters to life.

First time novel writers invariably live three lives – their full-time job, their friends and family commitments, and their novel. Even if you have a private income or are retired, juggling your other commitments as well as devoting time to your novel is still challenging. Whatever your circumstances you'll need to be committed, otherwise the novelty of writing the novel will soon diminish.

Although writing your novel will be time consuming, every day you have pockets of spare time that you can use to develop and shape your ideas – on public transport, waiting at the doctor's or sitting in the traffic. Use this valuable time – carry a spiral bound notebook and jot down ideas, or record them on your mobile phone or similar electronic device. In that way you'll keep your sub-conscious mind ticking over and focussing on your novel.

It's a technique used by British writer John le Carré. "I love writing on the hoof, in notebooks on walks, on trains and cafes, then scurrying home to pick over my booty."[1]

My Experience

Having completed *Uncommon Enemy*, I decided to share my experiences with others in the hope that it would help to inspire them to pick up a pen or turn on their computer. There are many books and websites available for aspiring writers but they often talk in general terms. *Writing Your First Novel* has a specific focus.

---

1. John le Carré, *The Pigeon Tunnel*, Penguin Books, London, 2016

No, I'm not claiming that *Uncommon Enemy* is the epitome of literary excellence. I know it's a good yarn because plenty of people have told me so. Obviously I'm also very familiar with its content – how each of the sentences, paragraphs, pages and chapters originated, changed, developed and were completed. To illustrate these points I've quoted extracts from *Uncommon Enemy*. In this edition I've also used extracts from my second novel *Robyn Hood Outlaw Princess*. Read the extracts with a critical eye. If they help you improve your own writing, that's great. If you can improve on my style, that's even better.

This book is based on my personal experience. Over the years I've done plenty of writing, including academic papers, two textbooks, song lyrics, storylines and dialogue for four musicals, radio and film scripts, and a doctoral thesis – and during this time I constantly toyed with the idea of writing a novel.

Nothing Comes out of Nothing

Several years ago, in a second hand bookshop I picked up Robert Harris's novel *Fatherland*. It was set in Nazi Germany in the 1960s, and was obviously a work of fiction as it was based on the premise that Hitler and his legions had won World War Two and the Nazi regimes still continued. The book made a considerable impression on me and I decided to adapt Harris's idea into a New Zealand setting.

Although there is unlimited scope for originality, many ideas are developed from the ideas of others. Consequently, when considering your first novel there's no reason why you shouldn't do what I did – use an existing novel as a way of getting started. One of my favourite New Zealand movies is Roger Donaldson's first feature film *Sleeping Dogs*, based on C.K. Stead's novel *Smith's Dream* – which tells the story of the establishment of a totalitarian regime in New Zealand. Harris's novel gave me that original concept and from there I considered combining the scenarios of the Stead book and Donaldson film as the basis for a novel.

So I was off – in pursuit of my dream.

Easy to write. Easy to say. Yet it took me five years to complete *Uncommon Enemy*.

During the first summer I attended a weekend writers workshop at the Centre for Continuing Education at the University of Auckland. By then I'd written several chapters of my first draft and had no idea whether or not they had any merit. The workshop required each of us to read an extract to the class. The positive response to my extract from the tutor and the other participants, and the ideas I gleaned from the workshop were enough to encourage me to keep me going.

Writing workshops and short courses are available in most towns and cities, as are on-line writing courses. They can be very valuable for aspiring writers so my advice would be to locate and enrol in one.

My novel was written in my spare time, evenings, weekends and holiday periods – more about this process shortly. Yet, in spite of the commitment of time and energy, it was very much a labour of love. Why? Because I wanted to do it, I was motivated to do it. My life and my living didn't depend on writing it, so any pressure I was under was entirely of my own making.

Writing *Robyn Hood Outlaw Princess* had a different origin. Some time ago I had co-written it as a musical with local composer Gary Daverne. Over the years many schools and theatre groups have staged the musical nationally and internationally and a year ago I decided to attempt to adapt it as a novel – easy to write, but harder to accomplish. Storylines in musicals are fairly thin as the music plays a vital role in showing the emotions of the characters. Consequently I had to expand the storyline, expand the characters, add new incidents, more action and danger, and a touch of romance.

I'd also joined the Mairangi Writers, a local writing group that meets regularly to read and critique each other's writing. I found this process invaluable in helping me develop the novel. It would certainly be worth your while checking out local writing groups.

2

WRITE WHAT YOU KNOW

Whatever we conceive well, express clearly. — *Nicolas Boileau*

The safest and easiest way to start is to base your novel on your own knowledge and experience. Yes, you may think it would be exciting to set your story in pre-European Africa at the time of David Livingstone, or the Parisian slums at the time of the French Revolution, but unless you have a considerable depth of knowledge about the place and the time period, I would advise against it. You'll have to spend a great deal of time researching the language, culture, events, people, environment and climate in order to create credible characterisations and a convincing plot – a process that you could find to be frustrating and time consuming. Yet, if you don't invest the time in research, your novel will run the risk of being superficial or at worst, somewhat farcical.

My Background

I grew up in Takapuna, on Auckland's North Shore – before the Auckland Harbour Bridge brought radical change to a relatively small and quiet part of Auckland. In writing *Uncommon Enemy* I drew on many of my personal memories and experiences to develop the events and the settings. One of my earliest memories for example was the blacksmith's shop in Takapuna where a bank now stands. Further north was Albany – a rural area where we went to pick apples from the large numbers of orchards – now subsumed in the urban sprawl. Prior to the building of the harbour bridge I made many trips in the family car on the vehicular ferry, and on the coal-powered passenger ferries. I drew on these memories when creating various settings for *Uncommon Enemy*.

I also have a long association with the University of Auckland and Auckland city itself and consequently was able to create a variety of scenes in and around these areas.

In 1965, while working in England as a schoolteacher, I drove a Mini from London to Warsaw over a 6-week period – a challenging trip that involved spending a month in Poland and East and West Germany. Subsequently I undertook a History degree – completing a number of papers on Nazi Germany and the Cold War. I also lived and worked in Southern Africa and over recent years have made several trips to Europe where, during my travels, my novel was constantly at the back of my mind.

Totalitarian regimes have always intrigued me, having had first hand experience of them in Eastern Europe and Africa. The various ways in which people have opposed or accepted them has been a continuing source of interest for me, and I have read widely and seen many films on the subject.

In short, I drew on my own knowledge and experiences, on the people and places with whom I'd come into contact – knowledge and experiences that I'd enjoyed or been challenged by – key factors in the development and enjoyment of writing *Uncommon Enemy*.

Robyn Hood Outlaw Princess, although based on a legend, had an obvious twist inasmuch as Robin Hood was now a female. Interestingly, my experiences with totalitarian regimes also influenced me in developing the musical and then the novel. Democratic governments and basic human rights were not a major feature of medieval England!

Draw on Your Own Experiences

So, in writing your first novel, draw on your own experiences or the people, places or events that really interest you. I spent a good deal of time travelling, but this is not a prerequisite for an aspiring novelist. If you grew up in a provincial town or have spent time in another country, consider using that as the main setting. Maybe your workplace could be incorporated into your novel – even the most mundane place of employment can be used to develop a plot or characters. It doesn't have to be in a royal court, a battlefront headquarters or the boudoir of some exotic temptress. Many a good yarn has been set in seemingly ordinary places.

Maybe an incident in your childhood or later in your life will provide you with the basis for your story. You can, of course, adapt or embellish it – after all you're writing a work of fiction. But if you were personally involved in the situation then you have the advantage of knowing how you and others felt about and reacted to it. Consider the English novelist Jane Austen whose books such as *Pride and Prejudice* have sold millions. She never left her native land, remaining within the confines of rural England. Yet her acute observations of men and women, their conflicts and foibles still resonate with people the world over.

Remember, even the most ordinary people have their secrets, their sexual longings, and significant incidents in their lives. It's all part of the stuff of life and provides rich pickings for the aspiring novelist.

What Appeals to You?

For your first novel you're best to select a genre that appeals to you, whether it's a western, a thriller, a murder mystery, science fiction, fantasy or a romance. Love of the genre will help to motivate you.

There are a variety of basic novel genres including:

Romance: Generally follows the tried and tested formula in which a couple meets, chemistry is obvious, tension and setbacks develop, but all is resolved in romantic/ passionate climax.

Fantasy: Generally some form of heroic adventure in which a hero who, in spite of a number of setbacks, confronts the forces of evil, wins through in the end and is rewarded with the love of a beautiful woman.

Science Fiction: Technologically or scientifically based with a variety of settings and strong characters. Plausibility is crucial.

Thriller: Hero (protagonist) is larger than life, who comes up against a villain (antagonist). Through great daring and bravery that overcomes seemingly impossible odds the protagonist wins through.

Murder Mystery/Whodunit: Made famous by writers such as Agatha Christie and New Zealander Ngaio Marsh, and provides a challenge to readers to identify the murderer from a variety of contrasting characters.

Crime: Similar to the Whodunit but covering a wider range. American crime fiction tends to contain more violence and corruption than its British/European counterpart.

War: Although a war or specific battle is often the main setting, invariably the story revolves around contrasting characters and the way in which the major conflict affects their lives. Love stories set in wartime also have considerable potential.

Humour/Satire: Always a challenge as what appeals to you may not be apparent to your reader. However, if you have an inclination then it's worth a try. Here's a title to get you going: *Nifty Shades of Grey*.

Historical Novel: Set in a specific historical era and draws upon the styles of other genres. It can include real and fictional historical characters – Robin Hood was almost certainly a fictional character, but the city of Nottingham had a sheriff, and England had a king, so, as is common in historical fiction, I mixed the real with the imaginary.

> *To the creative writer, fact is raw material, not his taskmaster but his instrument, and his job is to make it sing. Real truth lies, if anywhere, not in facts but in nuances.*[1]

Write your novel around an area or event that appeals to you, as the chances are that it will also appeal to your readers. After all, Tom Clancy had never commanded a Russian submarine but still managed to write the best-selling novel *Hunt for Red October*.

Another take on this theme is to write the kind of book that you've always wanted to read but could never find. Maybe it's unfashionable at the moment but fashions in the world of fiction are in a constant state of flux. Consequently, if your novel draws on a subject and creates characters that you'd love to read about, the chances are that others will also enjoy what you have to say.

---

1. John le Carré, *The Pigeon Tunnel*, Penguin Books, London, 2016

3

MAKING A
START

There is no lighter burden, nor more agreeable than
a pen. — *Petrarch*

Begin at the Beginning

Writers begin in many different ways. You may start with
a concept, an idea. You may have one or two contrasting
characters in mind. There may be a real or imaginary
event that's triggered you off. There's no right or wrong
way to begin, simply a diverse range of options.

At some point you'll need to decide to make a start. Some
aspects of your proposed novel may be crystal clear,
others rather hazy. However, if you've decided on your
genre and setting, read a selected number of books, and

made some notes on style, plot, characters, length, and climax that's enough to get you started.

You've allocated some time to make a start, checked your computer or collection of pens and paper.[1] So, what now?

The Inspirational Moment

You wait for the inspirational moment? Absolutely not! In order to undertake any form of writing, whether it's a report, a letter to a friend or a chapter of a novel, you've simply got to sit down and get on with it.

The business of writing requires you to write – it's as simple as that! So start writing. At the beginning? Probably, but if you've got an idea for an incident that will probably happen later in your story, that's fine. Write it down. Your main aim should be to put plenty of words on your paper. Yes, of course you'll revise and re-write them as part of the on-going process, but unless you've actually got something written, you've got nothing to work on.

Oh, and writer's block. This is often an excuse by beginning writers for procrastination. If you are feeling jaded and lacking in ideas, take a break. Do something different; weed the garden, mow the lawn or clean the car – then return to your writing and … write!

How Long Should It Be?

Most novels are between 60,000 and 100,000 words. Of course the longer your novel the more expensive it is to

1. John le Carré only ever writes with pen and paper

print so a publisher is likely to be put off by a blockbuster from an unknown author because the financial risks will be higher. For your first novel you should certainly aim for fewer than 100,000 words. (*Uncommon Enemy* is 90,000; *Robyn Hood Outlaw Princess* is 22,000.)

Perhaps you're thinking, "Sixty thousand to one hundred thousand words! I could never write that many." You'll be surprised how quickly your word count grows as you start to develop your plot and its characters, their adventures, encounters, challenges and relationships. Don't be put off by the seemingly large number of words. Begin your novel and surprise yourself!

And, once you start writing you'll set your subconscious mind in motion. You'll find that there'll be moments when a snatched conversation, a headline, a piece of film dialogue or a song lyric will trigger off the response of, "Hey, I could use that in my novel." Great. Make a mental, written or recorded note of it.

Time Management

Have scheduled writing sessions – plan times when you will sit down and write new sections or revise what you've already written. And make every effort to stick to your schedule.

Try to average about 4 pages per day (300 words double spaced). During weekends or holidays you'll be able to achieve more than this – setting yourself an average number of words will help keep you on task.

Double-space your typing. It's easier to proof read

particularly, if like me, you prefer to print the pages and go over them with pen in hand.

Pick a Place

Ideally you should have a place in your home where you do your writing, a place where, when you sit down, your brain says, "Oh, OK we're going to start writing."

Be Organised

I'm not the most organised person in the world but as I set about writing *Uncommon Enemy* I quickly realised the need to set up a system of writing and saving all that I'd written in recognisable and accessible files. These included research and reference material as well as my own writing because the sections and chapters were often completed and revised out of order.

The Opening Sentence

It was the best of times, it was the worst of times...

This is the first phrase in the opening sentence of Charles Dickens' famous novel *A Tale of Two Cities* – simple, strong, effective and memorable.

What do you think of this opening sentence?

> *Bill Thompson was born to Tom and Mary Thompson on 14 February 1951 in a small town just south of New Plymouth.*

Yes, it's informative. Yes, it identifies the character and tells you where and when he was born. Yes, it tells you the name of his parents. But it's dull and it's boring. The circumstances of his birth have the potential to provide you with the chance to develop some dramatic circumstances. Perhaps his father had deserted his mother. Perhaps her pregnancy had forced them into a shotgun wedding (it is set in the 1950s after all). Perhaps the 'small town just south of New Plymouth' was facing a crisis. Yet the dull opening sentence has merely given the reader a list of facts that are as exciting as reading Bill Thompson's birth certificate. You don't really need to know all these facts at this very early stage in the story. They can be developed as the plot unfolds, but not in your opening sentence.

Your opening lines should arouse your reader's curiosity, and draw them into your story. In *Uncommon Enemy* I began with an action sequence, designed to whet the reader's appetite and cause them to wonder, "Who are these people?" "Where are they?" "What are they doing?" "How did they get into the situation?"

> *The pair lay perfectly still. The Teutonic commands drifting up the valley were coming closer.*
>
> *"Dogs. I think they've got dogs?" she whispered.*
>
> *"Maybe." A distant growl supplied the answer.*

The reader knows nothing about 'the pair' or why they have to lie 'perfectly still'. Obviously they're in some kind of danger – possibly from German soldiers ('Teutonic commands') and attacking dogs. How does the reader find out more? They keep reading.

Here's the first page of *Robyn Hood Outlaw Princess* – set in a modern school playground.

> *"What are you girls doing?" The school principal was striding towards them.*
>
> *"Smelly, just our luck," whispered Janice.*
>
> *Reaching the group he hunched his shoulders and glowered at each of the four in turn.*
>
> *"Well?" he demanded.*
>
> *"Er, hello, Mr Smallfield. We're just on our way to History class," said Sophie, striving to adopt an innocent expression.*
>
> *"History." His glare increased.*
>
> *"Yes, History, Mr Smallfield. That's what she said."*
>
> *The principal stared balefully at the tall girl at the back of the group. "Robyn Howard, isn't it?"*
>
> *"Yes."*
>
> *"Yes, what?"*
>
> *"Yes, that's my name."*
>
> *The other three girls hurriedly stepped aside as the principal advanced towards Robyn.*

This opening scene was designed to show the bullying nature of the principal and the rebellious nature Robyn Howard. What will be the principal's response? Turn the next page and find out.

Check out some of the opening sentences from your favourite novels – particularly in the genre that you've chosen. Here's a selection of opening sentences from a number of New Zealand novels. What do you think of them?

> *In the world of political theory he was well versed, a democratic revolutionary cradled in the war filth of a Flanders trench'.*

John A. Lee, *The Politician*

> *Everything began from the moment I discovered the body on the beach.*

Kevin Ireland, *The Man Who Never Lived*

> *The art salesman at the bar, plying my friend Moppy with Tequila Sunrise, could become her lover.*

Diane Brown, *If the Tongue Fits*

> *Me and Fag was born on the double bed Mum and the old man slept in.*

Stevan Eldreg-Gigg, *Oracles and Miracles*

> *My father is dead and it is raining.*

Joy Cowley, *Classical Music*

> *January 1989. The passengers in the S-Bahn carriage seem inert from resignation. Riding a ghost train through a past they can never escape.*

Philip Temple, *To Each His Own*

The first time I saw John Heke he was no disappointment. Heralded by hoof beats and baying dogs, he rose shadowy out of the New Zealand forest on a misty midwinter morning.

Maurice Shadbolt, *The House of Strife*

The opening lines from my two novels had more action than these extracts as I'd decided that an action sequence would immediately attract the reader's attention and keep them reading. However other novelists begin their novels with leisurely, descriptive passages. Yet all are designed to encourage the reader to keep reading.

The Follow Up

Although I've quoted a number of effective opening sentences, they need to be followed with strong opening sections in order to sustain the reader's interest. One excellent example is from the opening section of Irish writer Iris Murdoch's novel *Jackson's Dilemma*.

Edward Lannion was sitting at his desk in his pleasant house in London in Notting Hill. The sun was shining. It was an early morning in June, not quite midsummer. Edward was good looking. He was tall, slim and pale. He was very well dressed. His hair, slightly curling, thickly tumbling down his neck, was a dark golden brown. He had a long firm mouth, a rather hawkish nose, and long light brown eyes. He was twenty-eight.

Note that the passage uses relatively simple language to provide a succinct description of the man and his immediate environment. The chapter goes on to slowly reveal further details of his birthplace, childhood and personal circumstances, thereby leading the reader on a path of discovery.

In another example from Murdoch's writing she begins her novel *The Good Apprentice* with a biblical quote.

> *I will arise and go to my father, and I will say unto him Father I have sinned against heaven and before thee, and am therefore no more worthy to be called thy son.*

From here she moves rapidly into a detailed scene involving the taking of hallucinogenic drugs.

Although the two openings by the same author are quite different, they both achieve the same effect – holding and retaining the reader's interest as the story and its characters unfold.

Here's the beginning of John Connolly's crime novel *Every Dead Thing*.

> *The patrol car arrived first on the night they died, shedding red light into the darkness. Two patrolmen entered the house, quickly yet cautiously, aware that they were responding to a call from one of their own, a policeman who had become a victim instead of the resort of victims.*

A simple but effective piece of writing. However, the author could have ended the second sentence after 'become a victim'. In my view the abruptness would have made a greater impact. What do you think?

Jonathan Delaware's crime novel *The Clinic* also employs simple writing, but with an interesting difference.

Few murder streets are lovely. This one was.

Elm-shaded, a softly curving stroll to the University, lined with generous haciendas and California colonials above lawns as unblemished as fresh billiard felt. Giant elms. Hope Devane had bled to death under one of them, a block from her home, on the southwest corner.

Notice how effectively the author contrasts 'murder' and 'lovely' in the first sentence. He then goes on to use positive adjectives such as 'generous', 'unblemished' and 'fresh' that again strongly contrast with the harshness of the final sentence.

English author D.H. Lawrence drew on rural England for many of his novels. Here's the opening of *The Rainbow*.

The Brangwens had lived for generations on the Marsh Farm, in the meadows where the Erewash twisted sluggishly through the alder trees, separating Derbyshire from Nottinghamshire. Two miles away, a church tower stood on a hill, the houses of the little country town climbing assiduously up to it.

Lawrence has made no attempt to whet the reader's appetite with a dramatic opening. Instead he's opted for skilfully using language to paint a scene in the reader's mind. Although adverbs should be used sparingly, his use of 'sluggishly' adds to the picture of the Erewash River. Instead of balding writing 'a church tower stood on a hill, surrounded by the houses of the little country town', he uses an active verb 'climbing' and the adverb 'assiduously' thereby not only creating a sense of relationship between the houses and the church tower but also implying a steady growth.

In writing your novel you'll have hundreds of thousands of words at your disposal to develop the plot, setting and characters that you hint at in your opening sentence and subsequent paragraphs. Avoid the trap of trying to provide too much information at the beginning.

4

YOUR PLOT

> Originality is nothing but judicious imitation. Most original writers borrowed from one another. — *Voltaire*

Plot or Character Driven

Obviously your novel will have a plot and within that plot your characters will carry out their activities.

In broad terms a novel can be driven by its plot or carried by its characters. Jane Austen's novels are primarily character driven. Although the plot contains twists and turns, there are no cataclysmic events. Yet the reader becomes engrossed in the personal issues faced by the contrasting characters and the ways in which these are dealt with and resolved. The characters are central and the reader enjoys following them to see how each one of them will react to their challenges and to the other characters in the story.

A plot driven novel is one with many twists and turns, unexpected setbacks and disasters. Frederick Forsyth's *Day of the Jackal* is one of many examples. In his novel the plot takes us through a maze of twists and turns, successes and setbacks as the assassin stalks his target, President Charles de Gaulle.

Plots and characters have symbiotic relationships – the plot tells the story of the events that impact on the characters; the characters show how they react to the events and to each other. Readers keep reading because they want to know what's going to happen next.

Some genres have a greater emphasis on one than the other – typically mysteries, crime and suspense are more plot-driven than romantic fiction. Whether you decide that your novel is to be plot or character-driven, remember that it is not an all or nothing, or a 50/50 situation. Your novel will contain a portion of both – the decision as to how much will ultimately be yours.

The Plot

For many writers this is the most challenging part of novel writing. Some writers prefer to predetermine the plot before they begin writing. Once they have decided on the beginning, middle and end of their plot they then proceed to write about the events and the characters. American writer Katherine Anne Porter (*Ship of Fools* – 1962) is adamant that, "If I don't know the ending of a story I couldn't begin." Once the planning of the plot is completed, such authors then proceed to flesh out the details in terms of scene setting, descriptions, action and dialogue – rather like a road map.

Unknown Destination

This didn't happen in my case. In fact I wrote six different endings to *Uncommon Enemy* and still wasn't happy with any of them. It was only when I went back through the story and, in order to add a twist or two to the plot, I added two more characters, German girls Gretchen and Sophie. Their interaction with other characters enabled me to incorporate them into an ending designed to create tension, a twist and a resolution.

By all means consider a destination at the end of your road map, but like any journey of your own choosing, you can always change your mind.

Initially I had a fairly loose concept. Yes, it would be an alternative history in which Nazi Germany would win WWII and New Zealand would be occupied. The main protagonist would be an Auckland university student and there would be a romance that would become complicated by the occupation. Press censorship would be imposed and the academic freedom of the universities would be curbed. With this very broad-brush sketch of the novel I began writing. The first chapter was designed to arouse the reader's curiosity and, although at one stage I actually deleted it, in the end I decided that my original idea, a flash forward, worked and I therefore reinstated it.

At the risk of sounding pretentious, much of the plot wrote itself. On a number of occasions I would allocate a morning to work on the novel and, apart from comfort stops and coffee breaks, would spend several hours at my computer. At the end of the session I would sometimes sit back and say, "How intriguing. How did we get here?" For example I began a chapter with Stuart, Carol, Brendan and Susan taking the bus to Albany and eventually rendezvousing with the guerrilla group. Yet, as I tapped away at the keyboard, I found myself describing a roadblock, a bus search, a confrontation with the New Order troops, the shooting of an officer, and an escape.

This does not mean that what I'd written was set in stone. Absolutely not! Having been intrigued as to how the plot had developed I then proceeded to re-read and re-examine the scene in detail, revising every descriptive phrase and sentence and every line of dialogue spoken by the scene's participants. Yes, it's great when the plot unfolds in front of you, but a careful evaluation of what you have written is still a crucial part of the process.

Robyn Hood Outlaw Princess had already been written – but as a plot within a musical. When I began to re-write it as a novel, like my experience with *Uncommon Enemy*, I also intrigued as to how the characters developed more breadth and depth, which in turn suggested areas where the storyline could also be expanded. At one point, to illustrate the cruelty of the authorities, I included a public execution by burning at the stake – my research for this chapter was a less than pleasant experience.

Pacing

Pacing is important. Vary your chapter and your sentence lengths as this adds variety to your novel. As a general rule, when writing conflict sequences (both physical and emotional) keep your sentences short and snappy. Use longer sentences for descriptive passages.

Twists and Turns

Early criticisms of the first drafts of *Uncommon Enemy* included a comment that the plot was too linear. By a third of the way through the plot the good guys and the bad guys had been established and in a series of encounters, they battled for supremacy. The action and descriptive sequences drew favourable comment but the plot was too predictable.

It was at this point that I added Sophie and Gretchen. They created doubt and unease. They were with the German occupation forces but offered to secretly ally themselves with the local resistance group. To build the tension, I had Susan regard them with considerable suspicion.

Brendan and Susan, having rendezvoused with Gretchen and Sophie, had just escaped an encounter with a German officer who had tricked Gretchen into speaking German. The four of them had barely managed to escape and were attempting to explain the incident to Jim, one of the resistance group members.

"What happened?"

"The German language and the inability of some people to keep their mouths shut!"

The vehemence in Susan's voice caused Jim to turn and face her.

"Explain."

"Just take it easy, Susan," interrupted Brendan. *"I'll explain slowly so that Sophie can translate for Gretchen."*

"These are the two German women from the White Rose?"

"Yes, I've—."

"Supposedly!" Susan's voice cut in. *"But the way they're going the only white roses we'll see are the one's that'll be placed on our coffins!"*

The scene is designed to sow seeds of doubt in the reader's mind. Later the two women were involved in betrayals and counter betrayals that reached their resolution in the final chapter.

No betrayals and counter betrayals in *Robyn Hood Outlaw Princess*. However, after she is captured by the Sheriff's men and thrown in jail, all hope seems to be gone. As Robyn explained:

It was late at night. They'd beaten me and I was in pain. Trying to sleep on the cold cell floor was virtually impossible, but eventually I managed to doze off. Then I was woken by the sound of someone opening my cell. It was dark, and I assumed the soldier standing in the doorway had come to beat me...or something worse.

"You must have been terrified."

"He advance towards me, and I was about to scream when-"

"When what?"

Robyn smiled. *"The moonlight shining through the cell window fell on his face."*

"You knew him?"

"It was William, the squire."

A Trouble Maker

Someone once wrote, 'A good scriptwriter is a troublemaker'. That's certainly true of a writer of novels. Whether it's an historical novel, a romance or a thriller, the plot should always contain troubles that have to be coped with, challenges that have to be overcome, and issues that have to be resolved. These troubles can be on a grand scale – the outbreak of war faced by all the *Uncommon Enemy* characters and their fellow citizens or the confrontations in Berlin during the 'peace talks'. The troubles can also be on a more personal level, contained within the larger problems – Carol's hidden secret, Hamish's childhood trauma, or Brendan's affair.

Similarly in Robyn's confrontation with the principal, a subsequent quarrel with her parents, her time travel to Sherwood Forest bringing personal doubt and uncertainty, her battle with the Sheriff's men, and her final capture and public trial – plenty of trouble and strife for the lead protagonist.

Maintain the troubles, the suspense, the 'what happens next?' as a constant thread in your story. Ideally every page should contain some form of doubt, problem or trouble.

Personal conflicts contained within larger conflicts are

in fact a common yet effective device constantly used by writers of fiction. A classic example is *Romeo and Juliet* whose personal love and resulting troubles are set within the broader conflicts between the warring Montague and Capulet families. Other examples abound – *West Side Story* (lovers from two rival gangs – based on *Romeo and Juliet*), *Gone With the Wind* (personal relationship conflicts between Rhett Butler and Scarlet O'Hara set within the context of the American Civil War).

You don't necessarily need to set your novel against a background of a major conflict. Conflict is a broad concept that can involve anything from inner conflict within the mind of a particular character, to a full-scale battle between opposing forces. Whatever form it takes, conflict plays a vital role in sustaining the story and in motivating the reader to keep turning the pages to find out how the conflict is faced and resolved.

Be Ruthless

You've probably been in the situation where friends are showing you photos of their recent holiday trip and, although some of their photos are underexposed or slightly out of focus they show them to you anyway – often accompanied by a detailed explanation. Although you smile politely in order to cover your boredom you're probably aware that the friends, having invested a considerable amount of time and money in their trip, feel justified in inflicting even their most mediocre photographs on you.

Be aware that the same situation arises with writers. Having spent hours, weeks, months on their book they often find it difficult to delete or heavily edit any passages because of the time and mental energy that they've invested in the writing. Yet, if you want to write a novel that others will enjoy you have to be ruthless in assessing your own work – whether it's incidents within the plot, the credibility of the characters, the vocabulary that you've used, or the validity of what you're trying to express. If it doesn't work, if it doesn't flow, re-write it until it does – or delete it! Mediocre writing, like out-of-focus photographs, will only irritate your readers.

5

YOUR CHARACTERS

Every man has his foibles, and often they are the most interesting things he has got. — *Josh Billings*

While the plot is of course crucial, it is the individual characters that play a vital role in involving your readers in the story. More than any other topic, we humans love to talk about other people – their faults and foibles and relationships. Therefore you need to ensure that your readers care about your characters, to sympathise and empathise with them, be delighted when the good guys overcome their troubles and achieve their goals, and be equally satisfied when the bad guys receive their just deserts. As the story unfolds your readers will gain increasing insights into your characters and their motivations through the way they deal with war, famine, pestilence and death or just plain old human relationships.

While your novel should have characters that your readers can relate to, beware of stereotypes such as the nagging mother in law, the self-righteous preacher, the mad scientist, the flawless heroine and the gallant handsome hero. Your characters can, of course, have many predictable characteristics. However, you also need to give them distinct and unpredictable traits, so that they are not merely cardboard cut-out figures.

Every character has to grow and change as a result of the events and the other characters they encounter in your novel. Strong characters make decisions in response to these occurrences – weak characters simply react to what happens. While the plot can be determined by the events, your characters can also determine its direction, by the conscious decisions they make at key points in your story.

The Chief Protagonist

In the case of Stuart, my main protagonist, I wanted him to grow and develop as he was faced with a series of increasingly complex difficulties. I didn't want to start with him as a sort of James Bond hero figure, who faces and overcomes every adverse situation with panache. I wanted to start with a young university student from a middle class New Zealand home who rapidly becomes faced with a series of challenges that he could never have imagined. By describing his home and family I was involving the reader in his life, enabling them to gain an insight into his character and environment and to identify with him as he subsequently faced each of his major challenges.

Schoolgirl Robyn Howard, transported back in time to be outlaw leader Robyn Hood, needed to grow and develop in her new role. After the first shock of realisation she enthusiastically takes on her position as outlaw leader, but is secretly plagued by doubt and fear. The way in which she reacts to each new situation provides the reader with fresh insight into the development of her character.

You need to give your protagonists flaws – they must have their doubts, fears, and setbacks before going on to overcome their mental or physical challenges. In some situations their personal flaws could put them in an underdog position – which will gain the sympathy of your readers. It's the humanity of your protagonist that will enable your readers to identify with them, to understand their problems while applauding their efforts to resolve them. In other words, to identify with them and care about what happens to them.

The Villain

While it's important to create conflict within and between the characters, it's also important to avoid making them two-dimensional. They shouldn't be merely all good or all bad. For example, in *Uncommon Enemy* Hamish Beavis was written as a sadistic, arrogant bully who cared nothing for anyone but himself. However, rather than simply show him as cruel and evil I extended the reader's understanding of him when, halfway through the story, he recalled the traumatic childhood memory of when his mother left him, never to return.

> *Struggling against his father's grip he stretched out his arms towards her. Looking into his eyes, she covered her mouth with her hand to mask a spontaneous intake of breath. She stood still for a moment and then she shook her head.*
>
> *"Sorry, Hamish. I've no choice." And she was gone.*
>
> *Bewildered he looked up at his father seeking an explanation or a word of comfort, but the man stood staring fixedly at the closed front door.*
>
> *"Bitch!" he snarled. Then he looked down at his seven-year-old son. "Don't ever forget it, Hamish. Like all women, your mother's a no good bitch!"*
>
> *He touched his son briefly on the top of the head and turned abruptly away.*

Although I wanted the reader to continue to dislike Hamish I also wanted them to gain a greater understanding of him as a character, to provide a credible background that would account for his villainous actions and, as the book progressed, to relate their knowledge of his childhood difficulties to his subsequent behaviour.

As *Robyn Hood Outlaw Princess* is a shorter novel I decided not to delve too deeply into the character of the Sheriff of Nottingham. The chapter that begins in the dining room of Nottingham Castle introduces him to the reader and provides an insight into his character.

> *Sounds of laughter and jeering floated up to the dining*

room of Nottingham Castle where its chief resident, the Sheriff of Nottingham, was commencing his lunch.

"What's that infernal noise?" he enquired of his chief steward.

"No idea, my Lord Sheriff," replied the man with exaggerated courtesy.

The Sheriff snapped his fingers and pointed to the goblet on the table in front of him. For the third time the chief steward filled it to the brim with red wine.

"Would you like me to enquire, sir?"

The Sheriff paused in the act of spearing himself a generous portion of meat.

"Do that. I'm not used to hearing laughter at this hour, or any hour in fact."

From this short scene the reader now knows that the Sheriff is rude to his servants, demands instant obedience, has a drinking problem, is greedy, and finds laugher and enjoyment abhorrent. Quite the charming fellow!

Your villain should also exhibit strength of character, an ability to manage and manipulate situations and people to achieve his or her goals – and, as your story unfolds, these goals should be achievable in order to create uncertainty as to the outcome of your plot.

Contrasting Characters

Your characters must be contrasting. No reader will turn

the pages of a novel in which all the characters are similar. While the chief protagonist is crucial it is the 'supporting cast' that inject lifeblood into your novel. In *Uncommon Enemy* I made an effort to create characters that shared similar backgrounds and values, but still had character differences – just like your friends or the people you work with. Thus Brendan, a friend of Stuart's is a more devil-may-care character. This is shown when Stuart first introduces him to Carol.

> *"Introduce me, old chap," murmured Brendan his eyes fixed on Carol.*

> *"Oh, yes, sorry. Carol, this is Brendan. Brendan, Carol."*

> *"Enchante, m'selle," murmured Brendan rising smoothly to his feet and reaching for her hand.*

> *Stuart quickly recovered himself. "Brendan's done a French paper. It's his subtle way of letting you know."*

A full description of the key protagonists is eventually important but do this sparingly, particularly at the outset. Give your readers room to create their own images of the characters, otherwise you'll not only overwhelm them but also leave them with very little else to discover about the person or the reasons for their actions.

All your characters, whether major or minor, should have a reason for being in your story. If they're going nowhere, or have served their useful purpose, eliminate them! After all, their demise (mysterious disappearance, death, murder, escape) has the potential of adding an intriguing twist to your tale.

Empathy not Sympathy

You don't have to like your characters but you must empathize with them – like Hamish Beavis, understand why they act and react the way they do. Invest some time in each of your characters – get to know their physical characteristics, background, upbringing, beliefs, and events that have shaped their lives, their goals, and their internal conflicts. Even if some of these aspects (sometimes referred to as the 'back story') do not appear in your novel you should be aware of them as they will assist you in adding depth to your characters by their speech, actions and reactions. Be aware, however, that empathy is not sympathy. Even if you've developed empathy for your villain, don't waste your sympathy by saving him from the fate that he richly deserves. Yes, Hamish's childhood accounted for his vicious personality but that didn't prevent me from leaving him to an unpleasant fate.

Even your relatively minor characters should have clear contrasts. For example, Stuart and Brendan learned of the invasion of Poland from D'Arcy, another university student whose bellicose attitude contrasted sharply with Brendan's pacifist views. Even though D'Arcy only appeared once in the book, his character was deliberately contrasted with Brendan's in order to highlight differing attitudes to the outbreak of war. Stuart, by quickly intervening and diverting D'Arcy's attention, is a third contrast in character in the short scene – hinting at the leadership qualities that he will show later in the story.

"Yep! It'll be off to fight the foe – for you two anyway," said Brendan.

"Whaddya mean?" D'Arcy looked puzzled. "If it's war we'll all have to bloody well go, like last time."

"We won't 'all have to bloody well go', mate. I'm bloody not. Didn't do any bloody good last time and it won't do any bloody good this time. War's a game for mugs. Let the politicians go. It's their fault, anyway!"

"Are you a bloody communist or something?" D'Arcy's face came closer to Brendan's. "We've all got to do our bit to defend ourselves and our country, and the empire, and—."

"Country! Empire! The Germans and the Poles are twelve thousand bloody miles away or hadn't you noticed? It's not our war. Let the Europeans get on with it!"

"You're a bloody conchie! You know what they did to those spineless bastards in the last show. Dragged them out to the front line and tied them to stakes. Bloody good show, too. Cowardly scum!"

"You're not including me in your 'cowards' category are you, mate?" It was now Brendan who moved his face closer to D'Arcy's. "And in any case, it took a lot of guts for those conscientious objectors to stand up against the mindless war machine that we created. So back off and think on!"

"OK, men, you've both made your point," said Stuart, easing himself between the glowering pair. "I don't agree with Brendan but he's right about the courage of the conchies. Anyway, D'Arcy thanks for the information. Hell of a way to end a day.'"

People You Know

For your first novel it's a good idea to base your characters on people you know. Maybe change their names or give them names that for you evoke positive or negative reactions. It then makes it easier to write about them as you can image that person behaving the way they do in the story. In *Uncommon Enemy* the character of Brendan was based on a close friend that I'd first met at teacher's college. Hamish was based on a combination of an obnoxious school prefect and an unpleasant workplace individual. Thus, as each of the characters confronted their situations, I was able to imagine the way in which the real life characters would have reacted. Inevitably of course, as your story progresses, the characters will develop and change, bearing only limited resemblance to the real life characters on which they were originally based.

Names

Anyone whose been involved in selecting a name for a baby will know that emotion plays a crucial part – similarly with the names of the characters in your novel. Choose names that have positive and negative connotations for you and then consider them in terms of your readers. Avoid names that sound the same – a pet hate of mine. They only confuse your readers, particularly when shortened versions (James/Jim, Penelope/Penny) are also used. There are thousands of first names so there's no need to have Harry and Harold falling in love with Harriet and Henrietta. The same rule, of course, applies to surnames.

Larger Than Life

This aspect is often contentious. In a James Bond story the hero is virtually invincible, the women he seduces are stunningly gorgeous, and the settings are often out of this world. If you're planning to write a novel in this style, that's your blueprint. However, in most cases, although you'll be writing about more credible characters, you could consider making them a little larger than life. After all, most readers of fiction want an escape from their own relatively predictable lives. Therefore, when they open a novel they're expecting something different, something that will take them out of themselves on an adventure.

Thus, in *Uncommon Enemy* I described the heroine, Carol as follows:

> *The young woman was even more stunning in close up. Introduced as Carol Peterson, her flowing black hair, stirred slightly by the wind, encased a face that was nothing short of exquisite. The rest of her was equally attractive. The fabric of the light floral frock flowed effortlessly around a figure that, while slim, filled out appropriately.*

Why did I describe her this way? Because I not only wanted Stuart to be instantly attracted to her but also wanted male readers to imagine the woman of their dreams and female readers to identify themselves with her.

However, to have Carol simply as a pretty girl with an attractive figure would have made her two-dimensional. Therefore, several chapters later when she met Stuart for lunch in Albert Park the following conversation took place that not only showed that there is more to her than good looks but also provided an opportunity for a reflection on the values of that time:

Carol rose slowly. "I have to go back to work in a minute."

"That was lovely. Lunch on the Grass, eh?"

"Yes," she said, "but not quite in the style of Manet."

"Oh." His surprise was genuine. "You know the painting?"

"Le Dejeuner sur L'Herbe," she said slowly and then smiled at him. "I loved art at school but dad said it was an entirely unsuitable career, so I became a secretary."

"And your mum?"

"She agreed. And in any case, she wanted me to marry Hamish. So a secretarial position was a chance to make a few pounds and fill up my hope chest."

Hamish was described as the cruel, heartless villain. I've never actually met anyone who is like Hamish but have read plenty of stories (authentic and fictional) that describe such individuals. Nazi Germany had more than its share of such unsavoury characters so I embellished the character of Hamish by adding a touch or two of Nazi villains such as Reinhardt Heydrich and Heinrich Himmler. Thus, Hamish's contemplation of his first Nazi Party function enabled me to show his perverted side (while at the same time dropping in the minor detail about the way in which cars were started at that time).

His immediate goals were clearly in sight but he would enjoy the anticipation a little longer. Carol wasn't expecting him until the following day and tonight he'd been invited to a Party function to welcome new members. A German member had smilingly informed him that the plentiful supplies of food, beer and wine would be supplemented by 'junge Mädchen'. He ran his tongue under his top lip, half-closed his eyes and felt a shudder of anticipation surge through him.

He turned on the key and reached for the starter lever.

"Young girls. How young?" he wondered aloud.

Rather than describe Robyn's appearance in detail I showed her as being athletic (captain of the First Eleven girls soccer team). I suggested that she was physically attractive when she was asked to the school ball by William Saunders, the captain of the school athletics team. Unfortunately for Robyn she let her temper get the better of her. She'd quarrelled with her Dad, arrived at school and had a confrontation with the principal, and had been sent to detention. It had all been too much for her, and she'd snapped at William.

William spun round, and without a backwards glance strode off towards the sports ground.

Robyn watched his receding figure until he turned a corner and disappeared from sight. Her mind was in turmoil. Her mother's let down, the confrontation and detention, and now a stupid argument with a boy she'd found interesting and attractive. She'd been surprised and pleased when he'd invited her to the ball, but her bad mood had got the better of her and now he'd gone. Tears of anger and disappointment filled her eyes.

Robyn was a leader at the school, but she was still vulnerable. She'd taken her anger out on William and as a result she wouldn't be going to the ball with him. She was the chief protagonist in the novel, but she had her weaknesses.

Naming of Items

Professor Sterling drove a 1937 Morris 12 car (three years old in terms of the story) that was in keeping with the character. An aging academic would be unlikely to drive a V8 Chevrolet even though they were common at the time. Naming items in your novel adds colour and provides further information about your characters and settings. So don't just use generic terms such as 'car' or 'chair' or 'building'. Include short details that add interest without slowing the narrative.

But be careful. In the first draft of Robyn I had her wielding a broadsword. However it was pointed out that a broadsword would have been too unwieldy and so I changed it to a short sword.

Character Change

In summary, each of your characters should be chosen for a specific reason, be clearly described, have a specific role to play and at times, specific tasks to perform. As your novel progresses the reader should be able to follow the changes in your characters so that when they reach the last page they can see the way in which each character has developed from the person they first met at the beginning of your novel.

6

YOUR
DIALOGUE

> Speech is civilisation itself. The word, even the most contradictory word, preserves contact – it is silence which isolates. — *Thomas Mann*

Dialogue serves a number of purposes:

- Breaks up the narrative
- Reflects a character's human side
- Displays a character's emotions
- Provides insight into a character
- Adds authenticity
- Shows character interaction
- Advances the plot

Dialogue should reflect the character of the speaker. For

example if a character found that someone was lying to them they could say:

"You're a liar!"

"You're a bloody liar!"

"You lying bastard!"

"I don't believe you."

"My dear fellow, surely you lie!"

"Huh, being free with the truth aren't we."

"Hang on, are you sure you've got your facts straight."

Each of the above examples would depend on the character and their situation. Although each line is a response to a lie, it is spoken in a distinctive manner, designed to match a particular type of character. Thus a ranch hand in a Western novel would be much more likely to call someone a 'lying bastard' than to respond, 'My dear fellow, surely you lie!' However, although your dialogue should match your character, it can also be used dramatically. A conventional middle class mother who called her son 'a bloody liar' would obviously be under stress as the phrase would be in sharp contrast to her usual speech patterns.

Dialogue should be succinct; essentially an intensification of everyday speech – free from the 'ums', 'like' and 'you knows' of everyday speech. Once you've written your dialogue, read it aloud to yourself or with a friend or two. It's a great way of checking whether you are writing natural or stilted speech, and for tightening up the flow.

Consider this example from *Uncommon Enemy* in which Stuart suggested to Brendan that they ask the soldiers they've just captured to come with them.

> *"Come with us, Stuart?" murmured Brendan. "You sure? It's a hell of a risk."*
>
> *"Yes, but as you've already said, we've got a distance and transport problem. Furthermore—."*

Bess pointed out to me that in a tense situation Stuart wouldn't be making pompous pronouncements. She was right, so I re-wrote it.

> *"Come with us, Stuart?" murmured Brendan. "You're sure? It's a hell of a risk."*
>
> *"Their truck'd be useful."*

Dialogue, while revealing more about the character and their interaction with other characters, can also add to your developing plot. In the following extract Carol described to Stuart her first sexual encounter with Hamish.

> *"Yes, but you still don't understand. There's more. You see we did it. He was satisfied but me, I was left frightened and, um, humiliated, by the whole process." She grimaced and shuddered. "I didn't enjoy it at all."*
>
> *"Not surprising, under the circumstances. Still it's all over—."*

"Listen to me, Stuart!" She was clearly becoming distressed but was determined to carry on. She looked him straight in the face. "I got pregnant straight away. Just from that one time."

"Oh. Bad luck," he murmured, realizing immediately the inadequacy of the response.

Dialogue should be taut and trim. Here are a couple more examples from *Uncommon Enemy* showing how I trimmed down the dialogue from the original draft.

"Jesus, Brendan. Don't you think that under the bloody circumstances..."

Stuart, at a loss for words, shrugged helplessly.

"Yes, I suppose you're right. Susan guessed of course. Women have an instinct for this sort of thing."

Stuart was obviously at a 'loss for words' so that phrase was removed. 'Yes, I suppose you're right', was unnecessary as Brendan obviously accepted Stuart's judgement of him.

"Jesus, Brendan, don't you think that under the bloody circumstances..."

Stuart shrugged helplessly.

"Susan guessed, of course. Women have an instinct for this sort of thing."

Stuart showed his pleasure at meeting Carol in Albert Park.

His smile was warm. "It's lovely to see you, Carol. Do you often come to Albert Park?"

In this case I trimmed the first sentence on the basis that it made Stuart sound rather wet.

His smile was warm. "Do you often come to Albert Park?"

In the scene where Stuart first met two members of the Fightback guerrilla group, the dialogue originally was:

"Just hang on a minute. Your instructions were on no account to bring weapons. You've not only disobeyed that order but have also brought a larger group, three of whom seem to be wearing bits of Jerry uniforms. They look like part of the Blitzkrieg Boys to us."

Too long winded, particularly in tense circumstances where lives could be in danger. I trimmed the dialogue and split it between the two guerrillas.

"Hang on. Your orders were no weapons. You've disobeyed that order and have brought a larger group."

"Yea, and three of them are wearing bits of Jerry uniform."

Stuart and the group move forward.

Setting the example Stuart moved quickly forward towards the end of the ploughed paddock.

I'd already established Stuart as the group leader and that they were moving forward in a ploughed field. Hence I trimmed the beginning and end of the sentence:

Stuart moved quickly forward.

Carol, waiting for a rendezvous in Albert Park.

> *She was still tense but the normality of the environment and the familiarity of the story calmed her somewhat.*

If 'the familiarity of the story calmed her' then it could be taken as read that initially she was tense, so I removed the first phrase.

> *The normality of the environment calmed her somewhat.*

Contractions

Notice that in many of the examples I've used contractions e.g. it's, you've, you're, don't. Contractions are typical of everyday speech so use them in your dialogue. There are times, however, when by deliberately not using them, they'll make a greater impact. Consider the difference between the following two sentences. It's much greater than the difference of the two extra letters in the second example.

'Don't do that'.

'Do not do that'.

Who's speaking?

Always make certain the reader knows who is speaking. It's comparatively easy with two people particularly if your characters have become familiar to your readers. In the following extract three characters are talking. But in the six pieces of dialogue it was only necessary to identify the speaker on three occasions. Read it through and see if you agree with the way I've written it.

He awoke to the sound of low voices. Carol and the man were sitting at the table. He coughed and tried to sit up.

"Take it easy, mate," said the man.

"You've been asleep for hours," said Carol coming over and putting her palm on his brow. You're still a bit hot but a long sleep is just what you needed."

"Yeah. I feel a bit better, but I'm bloody hungry."

"That's what we're discussing. We feel safe here and there's water nearby, but we've run out of food."

"If we stay here, they won't find us, but we'll probably starve to death," said the man with a grim smile.

"So we think we've really got no choice but to try to find the farmhouse. Geoff thinks he knows which one it is."

Each of your characters should have his or her distinct voice. For example Professor Sterling, an older academic spoke in more formal, measured tones.

As Stuart began to collect his papers the professor touched him on the shoulder.

"Young man, I wonder if you would be so kind as to wait behind after the others have gone. I'd like a word."

Now consider this example from Douglas Kennedy's *The Pursuit of Happiness* set in post World War II New York. Sara Smythe is negotiating an alimony settlement with her ex-husband George's family lawyer.

He was already scribbling figures on his desk blotter. "Twenty-five thousand two hundred dollars," he said.

"Precisely."

"It's a large sum."

"Not if you consider that, all going well, I should be alive for another forty-five or fifty years."

"That is a point. And is that sum simply an opening offer?"

"No – it's the final offer. Either George agrees to pay me that amount up front, or he can support me until the day I die. Are we clear about that, Mr Thompson?"

"Exceedingly. Naturally I will have to discuss this with the Greys ... sorry, with George."

"Well, you know where to find me," I said, standing up.

He proffered his hand. I took it. It was soft and spongy.

Notice how the author managed to convey the speaker with only a minimal reference to either or them. The 'he said' at the beginning established the lawyer as the speaker. Later Sara referred to him by name, a further reminder as to who is speaking, and of the formality of the occasion.

Notice how the hurriedly corrected reference to 'the Greys' was an effective way of hinting at George's domination by his parents.

The final two sentences are a simple way of completing the meeting while providing the reader with a further insight into the lawyer's character.

A point to ponder:

After Sara says, 'Precisely' the lawyer responds, 'It's a large sum.' Do you think the reply would have carried more weight if his reply had been 'It's a considerable sum,' or even just, 'A considerable sum'? I think 'considerable' is more formal than 'large' and strengthens the lawyer's guarded reaction to Sara's proposal.

Here's another example – from Vikram Seth's *An Equal Music* set in London. Like Kennedy's novel it is written in the first person, from the perspective of Michael the chief protagonist. In this scene Michael and Julia, former lovers, meet in a café.

> *There is a loud clanging somewhere, and the baby three tables down is yowling lungfully.*
>
> *"I'm sorry, Julia – this place is impossible. I didn't hear that."*
>
> *"For once—" she says, and I can read both tension and a touch of amusement in her expression.*
>
> *"For once what?"*
>
> *"Nothing."*
>
> *"But what was it you said?"*
>
> *"I'll have to tell you, Michael, sooner or later. It's better sooner."*
>
> *"Yes?"*
>
> *"I'm married." Softly she repeats it, almost to herself. "I'm married."*
>
> *"But you can't be."*

"I am."

"Are you happy?" I strive to keep the misery out of my voice.

"I think so. Yes." Her finger is moving in a small quadrant round the edge of her blue-and-white plate. "And you?" she asks.

"No. No. No. I mean I'm not married."

"So you're alone?"

I sigh and shrug. "No."

"Is she nice?"

"She's not you."

"Oh, Michael—" Julia's finger stops its movement around the edge. "Don't do this."

Notice how the author deliberately set the scene in a noisy café thus adding to the tension of the couple who are trying to discuss intimate personal issues. Like the previous passages the writing is relatively simple yet the tension is obvious. Occasionally the speaker of the lines is referred to and each time there is an additional phrase to reinforce the feelings contained in the dialogue. For example, 'softly she repeats it, almost to herself' hints at her doubts and ambivalence. The statement, 'I strive to keep the misery out of my voice' is simple and straightforward – there is a time for subtlety and obliqueness but in this case the frankness immediately conveys his feelings to the reader. When Julia asks, "Is she nice?" the question is ignored and the reply, "She's not you" reinforces Michael's feelings. Julia's answer shifts the conversation to another level and, while it acknowledges the tension between them, still leaves the reader pondering her true feelings for Michael.

Incidentally I liked the way the author invented the new word 'lungfully'. Says it all!

Slang

Speech style and patterns should always match the occasion. Sometimes this involves the deliberate use of slang.

The American writer Carl Sandburg defined slang as 'a language that rolls up its sleeves, spits on its hands and goes to work'.

Slang is often a colourful way of expressing ideas and opinions while providing authenticity to the characters. It is also a means of showing that a character belongs to a particular group or sub-culture. It is frequently colourful and a way of succinctly expressing attitudes or describing people or situations. In many cases it's linked with swear words – 'The poor bastard went deaf as a bloody post'.

As a writer you need to be aware that slang is constantly changing and that what may have been a common word or expression a decade ago is now out of date. Some slang expressions, such as 'cool', manage to maintain their relevance over a number of decades. Others, however, have a relatively short life span such as the noun 'wowser' (to describe a person who does not drink alcohol), now rarely heard.

Although slang is an informal type of speech, you still need to carefully consider its use in terms of appropriateness to the occasion, time and your characters. For example, a businessman at a 1960s board meeting would not say 'Not a problem, man'. Not only is this type of slang inappropriate for the more formal boardroom setting but the expression is also a relatively recent one. Thus, in writing the dialogue for *Uncommon Enemy* I was aware that the terms 'you guys' would never have been used in addressing men, let alone women, in 1940s New Zealand. It is the equivalent for that time of the now rather out-dated terms 'chaps' or 'blokes' or 'jokers'.

Similarly with swear words. Like slang they should be appropriate to the character and occasion. In a conversation between two soldiers under stress, 'fuck' would be appropriate whereas it would almost certainly be inappropriate in a lecture being given by a university professor. Like slang, swear words change their meanings and their level of acceptability over time. A good local example is 'bugger' which was unacceptable in polite society but in New Zealand has now come into common usage as the result of its endorsement by a TV commercial.

When writing slang or swearing use it to add impact, to expand the character and their feelings, or to authenticate the time and setting. Overuse will only irritate your readers.

Dialect or Accent

Some of your characters may have a dialect or accent

that is typical of their region (London Cockney, New York street kid etc) or because English is their second language. When trying to reflect this type of speech it's better to do so through vocabulary rather than a phonetic representation, which is only likely to confuse your readers.

Robyn, although set in medieval England, was written for modern readers. Consequently I had to ensure that the dialogue flowed smoothly but still retained the flavour of the period. In the following scene Sir Guy of Gisbourne, who is a henchman of the Sheriff of Nottingham, has been surrounded by Robyn and her outlaws.

> *"Presumably you'll be that foul wench Robyn of the Hood." In spite of his predicament his voice was self-assured and arrogant. Scornfully he surveyed the circle of outlaws. "A witches' coven, no less. Burning at the stake would be too good for you she-devils."*
>
> *"Raise your sword, Sir Guy of Gisbourne. We shall see if the quality of your mettle matches the foulness of your mouth."*
>
> *The flat of Robyn's sword smacked sharply into his left arm causing him to curse and recoil.*
>
> *"See, Sir Guy. Wenches can sting."*

Words like 'foul', 'wench', 'coven' 'she-devil' 'mettle', were common at that time. Although not used widely today, their meaning is still clear, thus ensuring that modern readers could follow the dialogue while maintaining the sense of another time and place.

When the German characters in *Uncommon Enemy* speak English, even if they are fluent, I still had to maintain a more formal way of speaking that is common to all speakers of a second language with which they are not totally comfortable.

In the case of characters like the German occupation official Schroeder, whose English was poor, I still had to ensure that his dialogue was comprehensible to the reader.

> *The large German grunted. "I see that you have nothing to say! That is good! You look and you listen and you learn, ja?" He chuckled at his own eloquence. "Now I take this man with me. He will be lesson learning, ja? And you will all be a lesson learning. Ja, I am thinking so!" He tugged at Stuart's shoulder. "Come, you stupid Kivi. Now I will take you to the Stationmaster's office. I wish to start your lessons soon!"*

Here's a good example of contrasting dialogue from John Fowles' novel set in the 19th century, the *French Lieutenant's Woman*. Charles Smithson and his servant Sam are visiting the English countryside.

> *Charles wished he could draw. Really, the country was charming. He turned to his man.*
>
> *"Upon my word, Sam, on a day like this I could contemplate never setting eyes on London again."*
>
> *"If you goes on a-standin' in the hair, sir, you won't neither."*
>
> *His master gave him a dry look. He and Sam had been*

together for four years and knew each other rather better
than the partners in many a supposedly more intimate
ménage.

It is clear from even this short passage that Sam is the servant. His speech pattern contrasts with his master's and when he offers an oblique criticism, the 'sir' is an acknowledgement of his lower status. 'Upon my word' is a slang expression that has long gone but its inclusion reinforces the period of the novel. The final sentence enables the author to further expand on the relationship contained within the dialogue.

Body language

Body language, while important in its own right, is also often used in conjunction with dialogue in order to add impact and insight.

Carol in conversation with Stuart:

"In the end, one Saturday night when his father was out
at some Rotary Club function, I finally agreed, just to
stop him going on at me, really." She looked up at him
briefly and then looked back at the ground, scuffling her
feet through the leaves that had wafted across the path. "I
didn't really want to but he'd been going on for so long
and—."

I particularly enjoy writing dialogue and the way words and gestures can often say as much or more than long descriptive passages. Examples are all around you, so keep your ears open.

7

DESCRIPTIVE PASSAGES

Imagination is the eye of the soul. — *Joseph Joubert*

It's in the Telling

Crucial factors in your novel are the way in which your story is told and the way in which the characters are portrayed and interact with one another. Of major importance is the setting, the environment in which the events, actions and interactions take place. Dramatic and traumatic events, conflicts and confrontations can happen in bedrooms or on battlefields, in parlours or palaces, on the factory floor or in a fantasyland. The challenge for you in your descriptive passages is to create a clear picture of each setting in the mind's eye of your readers – whether it's an untidy student flat or an emperor's throne room. Each contributes to the telling of your story, while your readers create their own picture of the time, the place, and the people in it. The setting enhances the key actions in the story, and frequently determines the ways in which your characters can act or interact within the confines or opportunities provided by each environment.

Although your novel needs to tick along at a good pace there are always places for well-crafted descriptive writing, particularly if it adds to your reader's understanding of the environment in which the characters are placed. 'Theatre of the mind', a term I emphasize with my radio broadcasting course students, is a relevant concept to bear in mind as you write a descriptive section. Regardless of length, each time you write a descriptive passage you should aim to conjure up images in the mind of your readers. I'm not suggesting that you drown your characters in a welter of flowery prose, but strive to create atmospheres and settings that add to your reader's knowledge of the place and their reaction to it.

In *Uncommon Enemy* I used a variety of environments. One was in Adolph Hitler's Reich Chancellery – obviously an ideal environment for tension and conflict. Other scenes of conflict (verbal and physical) were set in more common places such as Stuart's home and on the Auckland ferry. Don't feel that all your settings have to necessarily be in exotic or erotic locations. What's important is the ways that the events are depicted and presented within the environments that you've created.

Consider the following passages from *Uncommon Enemy*

– each set within markedly different environments. In the first Stuart's initial attraction to Carol is dampened because an older man accompanies her. As he sits morosely considering the situation, the passage paints a picture of the ferry crossing using active verbs, adjectives and nouns such as 'clattering...chains', 'familiar throb', 'steady pulse', 'wheeling seagulls' to create images in the reader's mind.

> *The other man gave Stuart a long stare. Then turning directly to Carol he lowered his voice and pointedly engaged her in conversation. The clattering of the chains as the gangplank was raised; the whistle from the mate as he unhooked the rope from the capstan and the clanging of the bells to signal the engine room, initiated the familiar throb of the ferry's engines. The steady pulse combined with the strong harbour breeze, the slapping of the water against the bow and the chatter of the other passengers made it hard for Stuart to overhear. Feigning indifference he gazed at the passing panorama of ships, boats, wharves and cranes and the inevitable wheeling seagulls as the ferry made its trip from Devonport towards the terminal at the bottom of Queen Street.*

Later in the novel a New Zealand 'peace delegation' arrived in Berlin. In this passage they were ushered into a room in the deep interior of Adolph Hitler's Reich Chancellery in Berlin. The description was based on pre-war photographs of the building and its interiors, a place designed to impress and at the same time intimidate all those who entered its portals.

> *From the Gallery the delegation was ushered into the large Mosaic Hall, assigned as the venue for the 'peace*

negotiations'. Around the tall marble walls pairs of giant grey eagles were inset into panels. At the opposite end an eagle with a swastika in its claws surmounted two huge mahogany doors. Men in suits met the delegates at the entrance. They directed them across a gleaming marble floor to a long table placed in the centre and covered in a heavy red and gold tablecloth embroidered with swastika patterns. Seating was provided on dark red Empire chairs, each decorated with the German eagle and the ubiquitous swastika. Slightly underlit and devoid of any natural light the area created an air of prescient foreboding.

Standing motionless at regular intervals around the Mosaic Hall were twelve SS Leibstandarte guards each holding a Schmeisser machine pistol in his white-gloved hands.

Signs of the German Occupation were appearing in all New Zealand towns and cities. This passage used the existing Auckland railway station building. The reference to the flags in the roof made use of adjectives and verbs and adverbs to create the image of 'slowly undulating shapes'. The reference to 'unpatriotic persons' suggested that the nation is not totally cowed by their conquerors.

The interior of the railway station had been similarly treated with large New Order New Zealand flags, suspended side by side with their red and black Nazi counterparts. Wisely the authorities had located them high in the roof, thus preventing their being ripped or torn down by 'unpatriotic persons'. Moving gently in the draughts created by the arrival and departure of the trains, they cast shadows on the upper parts of the walls. The effect could have been interpreted as picturesque but

for any who cared to look upwards, the slowly undulating
shapes created patterns of disquiet.

Nature with its myriad sights and sounds is a frequently used source for writers seeking to create settings and atmosphere. The opening of Liza Dalby's novel *Geisha* is an excellent example.

April in Kyoto is a glorious season. Cherry trees blossom
along the riverbanks and envelop the wooded
mountainsides in a thin pink mist. In Maruyama Park,
Japanese come at night to drink beer and sake under the
blossom-dripping boughs of an ancient weeping cherry.
The huge tree stands spotlighted in pale unearthly
splendour amid the noisy carousers.

Notice how the author made use of a number of adjectives, each one serving the purpose of embellishing her colourful word picture. For example, 'blossom-dripping boughs of an ancient weeping cherry' has three adjectives in a phrase of seven words (I'm counting 'blossom-dripping' as one word) – almost half the total. In many cases this would constitute an overuse of adjectives, yet, it this case it worked. In the middle of the passage the cleverly placed prosaic description of the beer and sake drinkers broke it up a little, allowing the author to then resume the lush language in the final section.

Barbara and Stephanie Keating made frequent use of descriptive passages within *Blood Sisters* – their novel set in post-war Kenya. Appearing early in the novel the following extract was designed to create a potpourri of images from the rapidly darkening African night.

The low rhythmic croaking of bullfrogs halted abruptly at the sound of Sara's footfall, starting up again when she stood still to breathe in the cold, highland air. The African sun had begun is slide down the horizon and she leaned against the verandah post to watch the majestic, red-gold retreat into earth. There was a chugging sound from the generator, a slow crescendo that brought with it the glow of lamps inside the house. Darkness always came so swiftly, with its sprinkling of early stars. Night jasmine and the scent of woods smoke masked the daytime smell of dust and gum trees. Beyond the protection of Lottie's garden, she heard the high bark of a zebra. Voices and laughter drifted out into the beginnings of the night to blend with the whirr and rasp of crickets and tree frogs. From the servant's quarters came the faint, tinny sound of a radio playing African music.

Notice how the authors mixed the two senses, sight and sound, with the actions of Sara to create the multiple images of the Kenyan dusk. Thus in the first sentence the sounds of the bullfrogs and Sara's footfall were juxtaposed with her action of breathing cold air from the highlands. Effective use was made of verbs: the sun 'slides' and Sara 'leans', and adjectives: 'majestic, red-gold' retreat into the earth. The use of 'retreat' suggested surrender, but by describing it as 'majestic' created a picture of a slow, measured transition from day to night.

Sensory language refers to words that represent sight, sound, taste, smell and touch. *Blood Sisters'* authors made appropriate use of this in phrases such as 'whirr and rasp of crickets and tree frogs', the 'chugging of the generator', the way in which 'smoke masked the daytime smell' and the simple but effective juxtaposition of sound and vision as the generator's sound resulted in the 'slow crescendo that brought with it the glow of lamps'.

Descriptive writing can also add impact to your novel's action sequences. For example I decided to set the final assault on the guerrillas' headquarters during a severe storm, using the natural elements to add impact to the confrontation. Rather than write a large paragraph describing the storm, I embellished each of the scenes with descriptive references to the elements, interspersing them with the reactions and dialogue of the characters.

For example in this extract, Stuart and Carol were about to walk from the woolshed to the farmhouse.

> *Stuart began to slowly open the door. Immediately it was nearly ripped from his hand by the crosswind. Lowering his head he stood on the top step and, narrowing his eyes against the wet stinging sheets, peered into the sodden gloom. Nothing suspicious was distinguishable and the only sounds were the periodic moaning of the wind and the constant rain tattoo on the corrugated iron woolshed roof.*

Hamish Beavis and his soldiers intercepted them.

> *Through the driving rain Stuart could see that Hamish was wearing a long black leather coat with a braided SS officer's cap featuring the death's head in the centre. He realized that the only hope of getting out of the situation was to attract the attention of the others in the woolshed. Drawing his head back slightly to relieve the pressure from the soldier's weapon he shouted above the noise of the elements.*

"Brave little pervert, aren't you, Beavis. Easy to abuse me when one of your minions has a gun stuck in my face. You wouldn't be so brave if it was one-on-one."

Stuart and Carol made a dash back to the woolshed.

A detonation of thunder buried all sound for a few seconds as the pair reached the woolshed steps. A flash of lightning momentarily illuminated the scene as Stuart, glancing upwards through the driving rain, saw several figures at the woolshed windows firing their Stens.'

The remains of the guerrilla group hiding underground.

By an unspoken consensus they had gathered in a group and seated themselves on the earth floor two meters from the bottom of the ladder. The moaning of the wind, the rattling of the windows, the unrelenting rhythm of the rain and the heavy footsteps above created a discord of foreboding that was reflected in the drawn features of the group as they huddled together in the semi darkness.

8

LOVE AND SEX

Love is a matter of Chemistry, but sex is a matter of
Physics. — *Unknown*

Describing in detail intimacy between two human beings
is often a difficult challenge for the novelist. After all,
even in these liberal times where sex is discussed openly,
personal details of lovemaking are not generally an
accepted topic of normal conversation.

Yet sex and love are human activities of crucial
importance and therefore your novel at some stage is
likely to require the characters to indulge in some form
of physical intimacy.

Such scenes should be integral to the development of the
characters – not just raunchy sex to titillate the readers.
The scenes should not only provide your readers with
a greater insight into your characters, their emotions

(hidden fears, guilt, passion) and their relationship with one another, but should also advance your plot – in terms of the difference which each love/sex scene will make to the future direction of your story and its characters.

An Important Distinction

It is important to make a distinction between sex and love. Sex without love is common enough – prostitution being an obvious example. In this case the coupling is a commercial arrangement between the prostitute and their customer. In other cases couples can engage in sex as a result of alcohol or drugs, or as a means to an end.

In Alice Walker's novel of the poverty-stricken Deep South, *The Color Purple,* the main character Celie's first sexual experience is of rape by the man she calls father. Walker's description, written from Celie's perspective, is one of brutal loveless coupling.

> *He never had a kine word to say to me. Just say You gonna do what your mammy wouldn't. First he put his thing up against my hip and sort of wiggle it around. Then he grabs hold me titties. Then he push his thing inside my pussy. When that hurt I cry. He start to choke me saying You better shut up and git used to it.*

Rape is repeatedly used in *The Color Purple* novel as a form of violence and aggression, and in doing so provides a depth of insight into the roles played by each of the characters and the poverty of their circumstances and their spirits. Walker's description of Celie's brutal experiences is in strong contrast with D.H. Lawrence's descriptions of lovemaking between Lady Chatterley and

Oliver Mellows in his famous novel *Lady Chatterley's Lover*.

> *He took her in his arms again and drew her to him, and suddenly she became small in his arms, small and nestling. It was gone, the resistance was gone, and she began to melt in a marvellous peace. And as she melted small and wonderful in his arms, she became infinitely desirable to him, all his blood vessels seemed to scald with intense yet tender desire, for her, for her softness, for the penetrating beauty of her in his arms passing into his blood. And softly, with that marvellous swoon-like caress of his hand in pure soft desire, softly he stroked the silky slope of her loins, down, down between her soft warm buttocks, coming nearer and nearer to the very quick of her.*

Wide Variations

Rape is a brutal sex act. Lovemaking, on the other hand, is a physical expression of strong feelings between two people. There are, of course, considerable variations between these two extremes. (Consider the controversy of E.L. James's bestseller *Fifty Shades of Grey* – described by some as 'mommy porn'.) Variations depend on variables such as the environment and the emotional circumstances. Yet always remember in describing scenes of sex and love that it is the characters themselves who are an integral part of the process, and it is they who determine the nature and level of the intimacy.

An example of one of these variations occurs in *Uncommon Enemy* when Brendan and Gretchen, the German young woman, have sex in the bush near the woolshed. The attraction was purely physical and it ultimately transpired that Gretchen was using sex as a means to an end. There were no preliminaries, no gentle foreplay. It wasn't rape, it wasn't lovemaking – it was just quick, urgent sex.

> *The rest of the sentence was stifled as her open mouth made immediate contact with his. For a moment he stood stunned then his hands slid in parallel up behind her back and cradling her head, pushed it more firmly against his. He felt her right leg slide over his thigh and the folds of her light dress brush provocatively against his bare legs. He moaned and quickly slid his hands down her back and under her skirt. He gasped as his hands encountered only bare flesh. Swiftly he lifted her upwards and in an instant response she locked her bare legs around his thighs and thrust her tongue deep into his mouth. Staggering a few steps off the track he sank on his knees into a nearby grassy patch where, with her legs still wrapped around him, he lowered her down.*
>
> *"Liebling!" was her single shuddering cry as he entered her.*

So, as the writer you need to decide if you are describing sex or love, or a combination of both. In doing so, consider the following questions – Does the love or sex scene advance your story? Does it provide your reader with greater insight into your characters? What sort of activity would be appropriate to the characters and their situation – raunchy and lusty, or slow and gentle? Will the lovemaking be wonderful and deeply satisfying for either or both or the participants, or will it result in doubts and fears – like life itself.

In *Robyn* I confined the male/female relationships to the early stages of a romance. Pip describes to Robyn what happened when Edmund, a young soldier, told her that he had to go north to fight.

> *"I'd long suspected he might ask for my hand. Now that he'd confirmed it, I too was terribly downcast. I started to cry and he took me in his arms and with infinite tenderness kissed me." She paused wistfully at the memory. "Robyn, it was the most beautiful thing that ever happened to me. Then we heard the perimeter guard coming so we had to part." She gave a long sigh. "God, how I miss him."*

As well as adding some gentle romance to the story the passage also shows that Robyn's band members were not anti-male, and that romance had been part of their lives and could still affect them.

A Standard Formula

A standard yet effective formula in fiction writing is for the lovemaking to take place after a series of setbacks and difficulties between the couple – boy meets girl, fall in love, quarrel, and make up. Sound too simplistic? Not really. As I said earlier, it's all in the telling. If your reader can identify with the characters they will want them to ultimately make love. Note that I said, 'ultimately'. Let your reader enjoy the tension of the courtship, smile at the growing attraction, become frustrated at the setbacks, worry at an apparent break up and ultimately join with them in the pleasure of climaxing the relationship – literally and figuratively.

Sexual vocabulary

One of the challenges of writing about sex and lovemaking is the way in which intimate body parts are described. D.H. Lawrence caused considerable controversy when he made direct reference to these hitherto unmentionables in *Lady Chatterley's Lover*. Now, although explicit sex is commonplace in literature and on the electronic media, it's still an area that needs to be written with care in order to convey the appropriate mood.

Here are some useful guidelines for writing about sex and love:

- Avoid using 'penis' and 'vagina' – they're more suited to health department pamphlets on communicable diseases. (Yes, I know D.H. Lawrence was biologically explicit but he's the exception that proves the rule.) Your reader knows the mechanics of sex so concentrate on the senses that are brought into play during lovemaking – tastes, scents, feelings, textures, and sounds.
- Foreplay is important. It not only provides you with the chance to explore and develop your characters and their relationship with each other, but also builds the anticipation in your reader's mind.
- Avoid euphemisms for nipples – they are what they are in their various shapes and sizes and it's OK to refer to them as such.
- Resist the temptation to use exaggerated euphemisms such as pleasure garden, love chamber, wand of delight, or rod of manhood.
- Sex is fun so, while avoiding the pitfalls of

inappropriate vocabulary, don't be afraid to show its amusing aspects – often a factor when couples grow more confident in their sexual relationship with each other.

- Use yourself to test the effectiveness of your sex scenes. If envisioning the scene that you are writing arouses you, then there's an excellent chance that you'll engender the same feelings in your readers.

- Describe the scene from the point of view of one of the characters. While you can show the other's reactions, it's simpler and more effective to stay with one consistent viewpoint.

- Use dialogue appropriately. Lovemaking is not a horse race and therefore doesn't require a running commentary. However, pertinent dialogue can very effectively heighten the tenseness, sensuality and expressions of love.

Lovemaking doesn't always have to end in successful shuddering climaxes. It's a delicate business, fraught with frustrations and pitfalls. Unsatisfying sex can be a very effective device in conveying insight into the characters or shifting your plot into a different direction

In writing scenes of sex and love always consider your characters as the prime determiners of the nature of the physical act and develop your description from that point. Oh, and when writing love scenes, enjoy yourself. After all, you're an active participant!

9

GRAMMAR, PUNCTUATION, PARTS OF SPEECH AND SPELLING

Grammar: A system of general principles for speaking and writing according to the forms and usage of a language. Collins — *New English Dictionary*

All words are classified as parts of speech. They are the tools with which you'll be crafting your novel. Put simply, the main parts of speech are:

Nouns – naming words

Park, university, girls, soldiers

Proper nouns -names of people and places are proper nouns and are always capitalised.

Albert Park, Oxford University, Germany

Verbs – doing words

Run, jump, laugh, complain

Finite verb – finite verb forms are namely conjugated verbs that show person, number, tense, aspect, and voice.

I go, she goes, he went

Non-finite verbs – have no person, tense or number

to go, going

Participles

English has two participles – present and past. They can also be used as adjectives.

Adding 'ing' to the base form forms the present participle – I'm leaving town.

Adding 'ed' to the base form creates a past participle – They've just arrived.

As an adjective – a dying man.

Adjectives – describing words

tasty, exquisite, deep

Adverbs – words that tell how, and add meaning and colour to the verbal action:

uncertainly, softly, inaudibly

A warning: Adverbs are very tempting, particularly if you're worried that the reader needs a little extra help to get the full impact of a sentence. However you should avoid adverbs unless they add value. A good test is to check how your sentence would read without the adverb. If the meaning hasn't changed then delete it. For example:

> *The knife flashed. "I'm going to kill you," he whispered quietly.*

Here 'quietly' is the adverb. Yet, how else would he whisper? How about 'he whispered menacingly'? Yes, but that should be obvious from the context. After all he has a knife and he's whispering, so it's obvious that he has menacing intentions. How about this?

> *The knife flashed. "I'm going to kill you," he whispered.*

In this case the adverb is superfluous. However, they do have their place.

Consider this opening adverbial phrase from *Uncommon Enemy*:

> *The pair lay perfectly still.*

I could have left out the adverb 'perfectly' but I wanted to emphasize that the pair had to remain as still as possible due to the increasing danger – hence the adverb.

Imagery

Touches of imagery add value to your writing. The similes and metaphors constantly used in conversation, although often full of clichés (flat as a pancake, thick as a brick, dead from the neck up) are used by all of us because we are aware that the imagery adds impact to what we're trying to express.

Similes: A simile is a comparison that uses the words 'like' or 'as' – as dry as a bone, swears like a trooper, drinks like a fish.

One of my favourite similes is from John Masefield's poem *Sea Fever* where

> 'The wind's like a whetted knife'.

Metaphors: A metaphor compares two dissimilar things suggesting that one thing is another – his bedroom is a tip, it's raining cats and dogs, life's a bitch. Shakespeare wrote that 'All the world's a stage and all the men and women merely players'.

Similes and metaphors frequently conjure up imagery. Use imagery in your novel but avoid clichés unless they fit the character or situation.

Writing Terms

Here's a list of common writing terms, some of which you may have forgotten from secondary school. They're useful in analysing your own work or in discussing it with and editor or publisher.

Allegory: use of a character or situation to express a wider truth

Alliteration: series of words in a sentence that all begin with the same sound – pampered pompous pig

Analogy: a comparison of two dissimilar objects to show similar aspects. For example the operation of a computer could be said to be analogous to the human brain.

Anaphora: consecutive sentences starting with the same group of words – The power of truth is pure. The power of truth is good. The power of truth will set you free.

Antonyms: words that have the opposite meaning: mean/ generous, fair/foul, beautiful/hideous

Cliché: expression widely overused – flogging a dead horse

Double Entendre: phrase that can be interpreted in two different ways – very common in saucy British movies and TV shows – "I'm going out for a bit."

Euphemism: a phrase used to disguise something disagreeable or unpleasant – she passed away

Homographs: words that share the same written form as another but have a different meaning: sow/sow, fair/fair, row/row.

Homonyms: words spelled and pronounced alike but that have different meanings – acts/axe, air/heir, aisle/I'll.

Hyperbole: deliberate exaggeration – I'm dying of hunger

Onomatopoeia: word that imitates what it stands for – smash, sludge, cool

Oxymoron: two words with contradictory meanings – a common one designed to get a laugh is 'military intelligence' – now rather a cliché.

Personification: providing living characteristics to inanimate objects – trees sighing in the breeze

Synonyms: words that have the same meaning – evil, villainous

Voice: in writing, this refers to how an author 'sounds' on a page – the style, the tone

Grammar and Spell Check

Poor spelling and bad grammar are unacceptable to publishers and readers. On no account hand your manuscript to a publisher unless you have thoroughly proof read it. A poorly proofread manuscript immediately suggests that the writer is sloppy and has no real commitment to his or her writing. Always get a second and even a third person to read it through. Remember, it's so easy for you, as the author, to read what you thought you put instead of what's actually written on the page.

Make full use of computer Spelling and Grammar Check facilities. No, they're not infallible, but they are very useful in checking your typos and offering you alternative ways of structuring your sentences or phrases.

If you're writing for British and Commonwealth markets

then set your Spell Check to English (UK). If you're aiming for the American market then the English (US) Spell Check is ideal.

A tip – if you're using foreign words or phrases and you're not sure if the spelling or grammar is correct, change your Spell Check to that language (e.g. German, French) and it will make the basic corrections for you.

Thesaurus

Whether on your computer screen or in printed form, a thesaurus should be close at hand as you write and revise your novel. It's a rich source of alternative ways of saying the same words over and over again, as well as providing similes, metaphors and phrases that will enable you to add variety to your writing.

Computer Literacy

Although Shakespeare wrote with a quill pen, I'm certain he would have revelled in the opportunity to use a computer. If you don't already have one, give it serious consideration. For speed, efficiency and sheer ease of operation, I'd strongly recommend purchasing a computer with a software package such as Word. (It's a tax-deductible expense for a serious writer.)

You can improve the quality and speed of your typing with one of a number of typing tutorials. They are worth preserving with, as the ability to touch type will enable you to concentrate on your story and characters – rather than using up your creative energies hunting and pecking.

If you're not particularly computer literate I suggest you enrol in one of the many short evening courses offered by secondary schools, community colleges, polytechnics or universities.

And always remember when using a computer – constantly save and back up!

Numbers

Be consistent with your numbers. As a general rule use words for numbers up to twenty and after that use numerals. However, always start a sentence with a word, not numerals – "One hundred dollars?" gasped Dan … not "$100?" gasped Dan.

Speech

Check how direct speech is written in other novels. Some authors move outside the convention and don't use speech marks at all. However, as a first time novelist I would strongly recommend you follow the conventions that are basically:

- Indent each separate piece of dialogue. (Make sure you've defined the indentation in the Paragraph section of the Format menu.)
- Use quotation marks for each separate piece of dialogue no matter how short – "Yes," she replied.
- Commas either prior to or after the end of a spoken section – Carol replied, "I'm sorry." Or "I'm sorry," replied Carol.

Layout

Rather than detail all the layout rules I suggest you check other novels as well as the guidelines often provided by publishers (frequently on their websites). Spacing, indenting, font sizes and styles are fairly standard and not difficult to follow.

10

ATTENTION TO
DETAIL

> Your novel is a work of fiction, but that doesn't mean
> that your facts don't need to be correct.

Few viewers of films pay much attention to the details
of sets (settings), whether in a Western bar, a Victorian
drawing room or a Californian lounge. Yet if details of
furniture, pictures, books, items on desks, floor or wall
coverings are missing, or are at odds with the period, the
dramatic effect would be compromised.

In your novel you have to rely on the written details to
paint a picture for your reader. These details are crucial
in creating the authenticity and believability that help
involve your readers in the story. In writing *Uncommon
Enemy* I drew on my own memories – for example how

my parents dressed and behaved. Other sources included the memories of older people who had served in the war, novels and history books, searching websites and watching period films. They all enabled me to glean details that would add to the authenticity of the various settings. The following paragraph, was set on the Devonport wharf during the 1939 morning rush hour.

Managing to push his way to the front, Stuart was the first off. Entering the terminal, he moved quickly through the crowd of men in hats, suits, sports coats and flannel trousers, and a sprinkling of military uniforms. The women, mostly in their late teens or twenties, or past marriageable age, were smartly dressed in knee length skirts or dresses with hats, gloves, and stockings as befitted those who worked in city offices and shops.

In some cases, it just involved my reading books and making a few notes. In other cases, such as the interior of the Hitler's Reich Chancellery, I studied a number of colour photographs and reading a description of the building and its settings. Although it was demolished at the end of World War II, my wife and I were able to walk around the area described in the book during a visit to Berlin in January 2005. It was a dark, cold day and for both of us the atmosphere of what had once been the centre of the Nazi web still lingered, evoking a range of conflicting feelings. On our return home I revised the Berlin passages in the light of what we'd experienced.

Minor descriptive details also add validity to your story. Consider these *Uncommon Enemy* examples.

Appropriate apparel for cycle riding:

He had to tell himself to slow down as he parked his bike, removed the cycle clips from around his trouser cuffs and headed straight for the group.

Cigarette smoking in the 1940s:

Finding a spot in the university library by a window he spread his notes out on the desk, lit a cigarette and began the task of completing the summaries he had been preparing in anticipation of the exam questions.

Transport and pub closures in central Auckland in the 1940s:

A tram, its bell clanging, rattled by noisily. The newsboy was doing a roaring trade and around him complete strangers were forming discussion groups – their tongues already loosened by the beer consumed at the pubs that had closed an hour earlier at six o'clock.

Stuart and Susan went to the movies. I knew what film was showing on that date as I'd checked the *New Zealand Herald* in the library archives – a valuable source of local history.

"What's on?"

"A musical, The Wizard of Oz. Do you like musicals?"

Similarly with *Robyn* I researched customs of the time, using paintings, photographs from plays and films and writing from novels. Here are a few examples:

There's a blood price on the head of all outlaws.

Wooden goblets were passed around.

Fluttering from the tips of their lances were red-and-blue swallowtail flags.

The scrivener hurriedly appeared with quill pen, ink bottle and parchment.

Historical Characters

The character of Nazi bureaucrat Hermann von Muller-Rechberg, although fictional, was based on my imagined character of a person working for the Third Reich whose superficial egregiousness would mask an unpleasant personality. However, in the case of real figures such as New Zealand Prime Minister Peter Fraser, I had to spend some time researching their background and personalities and then assess how they might have behaved at the Wellington meeting and in the Reich Chancellery situation. Several sources referred to Fraser as proud of being a self-educated man and a low tolerance for those who questioned his opinion. Hence, Professor Sterling's comment to Stuart and Brendan:

> *"As you know, he was born in the Scottish Highlands. His parents were not well off and he had to leave school at twelve and go to work. He immigrated to New Zealand and educated himself by reading extensively and involving himself in local politics. Eventually he gained the highest position in the land. Unfortunately somewhere along the way, he acquired a deep suspicion of academics."*

In the case of German Foreign Secretary Joachim von Ribbentrop, many members of the international community and his Nazi peers regarded him with a certain scorn. His acquisition of the aristocratic 'von' title through a contrived 'adoption' by a titled aunt added to my insight into a superficial character, for whom violence and betrayal were second nature.

11

CATALYST, CRISIS AND CLIMAX

> When written in Chinese the word 'crisis' is comprised of two characters – one represents danger, the other opportunity. — *John F. Kennedy*

The Catalyst

The moment when the chief protagonist is forced into action by circumstances constitutes a catalyst. In the case of *Uncommon Enemy* it was the start of a war. In other cases, it could be the murder of a loved one, a natural disaster, or a major loss at a casino. The catalyst creates problems and challenges because the protagonist loses some measure of control.

Early in *Uncommon Enemy*, Stuart was confronted with the outbreak of World War II.

> *"Late City!" cried the Auckland Star newsboy standing in his usual street corner spot. "Read all about it! Allies declare war on Germany! King George speaks to the Empire!"*
>
> *The Germans! He'd completely forgotten about them. Now they were poised to smash his hopes and dreams at the incubation stage.*

In *Robyn Hood Outlaw Princess* there are various incidents early on in the story. However, the main catalyst is when she finds herself in Sherwood Forest, dressed as an outlaw.

> *Sherwood Forest, outlaws, bows and arrows and a leader who wore a distinctive hood. Was she Robyn Hood, an outlaw leader of a band of women? Her heartbeat quickened with excitement as the idea developed. In spite of the price on her head, if this was some sort of new reality, she was starting to feel comfortable with it.*

The Crisis

At this point the reader usually knows the major characters and their backgrounds. Thus they are drawn into the issues faced by the character.

Your novel should contain a series of crises, large or small, imposed by external events such as the outbreak of a war, or personal problems such as a family death. Crises keep the reader involved as they empathise with the character and his or her reaction to a situation –

particularly one involving a crisis of faith in which they are faced with real doubts, fears and powerful emotions.

Towards the end of *Uncommon Enemy* Carol was coming to terms with the result of an assault on guerrilla headquarters.

Nevertheless her mind was a confused jumble of images, the strongest being that of Stuart's lifeless body in the carnage of the woolshed floor. As the truck continued its bumpy journey down the rutted road an inexorable ache of emptiness crept over her skin and crawled into every part of her being.

The reader will wonder and worry if your main character(s) will confront and overcome the crisis. At this point in your novel the crisis should leave room for doubt – if it's obvious that the hero/heroine will win through your reader will feel let down by a story that was 'too predictable'.

The trial of Robyn Hood in the Nottingham city square provided a crisis.

Intimidated, the citizens at the front joined in the chant. At first they mumbled but as the advancing soldiers knocked several citizens to the ground, others joined in and the chant grew in volume. Hysteria began to flow through the throng. Caught up in the rhythm and volume, they eventually joined in: "Guilty! Guilty! Guilty!"

"Prepare the gibbet!" ordered the Sheriff.

The Sheriff's triumphant smile filled her with dread.

Climax

The climax occurs when the forces and key characters confront each other and resolve their issues – often through strong dialogue or physical violence. It can be a major climax in which villain and hero battle it out in a James Bond style confrontation. Even if it's on a much lesser scale it still requires doubt and tension.

In *Uncommon Enemy* I had a series of climaxes as the book approached its conclusion. The final one involved a traitorous twist.

> *"Yes, in a manner of speaking." She laughed harshly and in a rapid movement reached into her shoulder bag and produced a small Walther PPK pistol. "Both of you stand back against the wall. Now!"*
>
> *"You traitor," hissed Carol.*

The Denouement

Borrowed from the French word meaning 'the untying' it refers to the dissecting or clarification of your story and hints at the future paths of your chief protagonists. Rather like a postscript or an epilogue, it's a common device in a novel, particularly when an ending has been violent or catastrophic. In the denouement, the climax and loose ends are resolved, and the tension dissolves. Your reader is shown that life after the climax still continues but in new and different directions. Thus they're provided with the opportunity to reflect on the events and to ponder the future as they close the book.

Writers down the centuries have used the denouement.

In the biblical story of the Prodigal Son, the son, having 'wasted his substance on riotous living' and then hitting rock bottom, tentatively returns home. His father greets him warmly and forgives him. In the denouement the father throws a party, invites his friends and other family members to join him in celebrating his son's return to the family, but the eldest son is less than pleased.

Another example is in the final scene in Shakespeare's *As You Like It* in which the couples are married, the evil doer repents his sins, the two disguised characters reveal their identities, and the ruler is restored to his rightful position.

Similarly, films frequently contain a denouement. A classic example occurs at the end of the Western movie *High Noon*. Sheriff Will Kane (Gary Cooper), having single-handedly fought the Miller Gang in a brutal gunfight is surrounded by the townspeople who all emerge from the nearby buildings. Disgusted at their lack of support he drops his badge in the dust of the main street and rides away with his new bride (Grace Kelly). In this case the denouement makes a strong comment on the key aspects of the plot, leaving the audience with much to contemplate.

In *The Color Purple* the closing paragraph of the final short chapter completes the denouement. After all the trials and trauma that she's experienced, Celie, having made reference to the key surviving characters, contemplates the future with optimism.

I feel a little peculiar round the children. For one thing, they grown. And I see they think me and Nettie and Shug and Albert and Samuel and Harpo and Sofia and Jack and Odessa real old and don't know much what is going on. But I don't think us feel old at all. And us so happy. Matter of fact, I think this the youngest us ever felt.

Romantic novels often have a straightforward denouement that extends and ties up the happy-ever-after ending in which a summary explains that the protagonists went on to live successful and fulfilling lives. However, even novels that contain a traditional happy-ever-after ending can still leave a hint of doubt to intrigue the reader.

In the case of *Uncommon Enemy* Stuart and Carol left the university grounds together. Although they had resolved their personal issues and were clearly in love with each other, together they faced an uncertain future. New Zealand was still under Nazi occupation and although at the end of a previous chapter I had suggested that Hamish Beavis received his just deserts, I didn't actually kill him off. Consequently the reader can ponder the fact that his presence may continue to lurk in the background.

Her voice was soft. "Just tell me again that we've promised to look after each other."

Reaching up he took her face between his hands.

"Yes, Carol, whatever happens I promise I'll always look after you."

The warmth of her smile was spontaneous.

"Me too."

As the chiming of a distant clock sounded a light rain began to fall. Hand in hand, they moved quickly through the university grounds and emerged on to the dark glistening street.

12

RESOURCES
AND SOURCES
OF SUPPORT

> I love being a writer. What I can't stand is the
> paperwork. — *Peter de Vries*

Some writers are adamant that they want no assistance
from anyone in the development of their novel. John
Connolly, an international writer of spine chilling
thrillers (*The Black Angel, Every Dead Thing*) was adamant
at a book promotion I attended in Takapuna that he
never, ever shows his work-in-progress to his family or
friends.

In my case I found the comments of family and friends
very helpful. This did not mean that I had to accept every

word of their opinions, but at several stages I ran off copies of the novel and asked various people to read it and make comments. I strongly emphasized that would do me no favours by saying nice things if they didn't really believe them. They were instructed to try to forget that the author was a friend or a relative and highlight what they saw as the main strengths and weaknesses of the plot and characters.

In each case, after they'd read the manuscript I discussed their opinions by phone or face to face. During these conversations I quickly realised that I had to avoid the temptation of trying to explain any perceived flaws or weaknesses. I had to make myself listen and note what they, as potential readers, felt. Long-winded justifications from the author served no purpose! This process assisted me in many aspects as I drew on as wide a range of opinion as I could – including my sons and one or two of their friends to glean an opinion from the next generation.

Some people highlighted errors while others provided additional information. In the first draft I had the Nazi atomic weapon being exploded on the south Atlantic island of St Helena. However a friend pointed out that it was out of range of a WWII bomber so I changed it to the Orkney Islands, and strengthened the impact by providing a link with Stuart's family.

He looked at his mother. "As your friend told you, the Germans dropped the bomb on the Orkneys to demonstrate its destructive powers. They've told the British they'll do the same to a city in England unless they surrender within forty-eight hours. He told us to listen to the six o'clock news from London tonight because he's pretty sure that Britain will have no alternative but to agree."

They all sat silently and then his mother began to cry. "My aunt often talked about the Orkneys – the kind people, their pretty fishing villages and wonderful historical sites. How could they?"

Others assisted with minor details such as the colour of the buses and the bus routes in wartime North Shore.

Earlier in the morning they had boarded the yellow North Shore Transport bus near the blacksmith's shop in central Takapuna and headed to Northcote where they had then caught the bus for Albany.

Another friend pointed out that the British Sten gun was a weapon favoured by all guerrilla groups fighting against the Germans:

They were also taught to load and fire some newly acquired Sten guns. The weapon, designed for close range engagements, was particularly useful to a group like Fightback as it could also be fired using German 9mm ammunition.

13

REVIEW, REVIEW AND THEN REVIEW AGAIN

> There is no royal path to good writing; as such paths as exist do not lead through neat critical gardens, various as they are, but through jungles of self, the world, and of craft. — *Jessamyn West*

Let's assume that you've finished your first draft, or have reached a point where you don't feel you can write any more. At this point it's a good idea to put your novel away for a week or more – particularly when you've finished your first draft. Coming back to it after a period enables you to take a fresh look at the writing, the plot and the characterisation. Re-read it with a pencil in your hand – or directly from your computer screen if you prefer. Carefully evaluate everything you've written – cleaning out or re-working unnecessary words or phrases.

For many writers this is their greatest challenge. They have laboured long and hard over their descriptive passages and dialogue. Consequently they find it very hard to revise, re-write or discard their work. They take the attitude that, 'It's my writing and therefore it's sacrosanct.' Not so, I'm afraid.

You need to be prepared to repeat this process many times as you review and re-review successive drafts until you're satisfied that your novel is as well written as you can make it. David Poyer, an American writer of sea fiction, sums the process up neatly. "Ninety per cent of a writer's skill is learned alone, trying to do the best you can, over and over, till it's as good as you can do – and you'll find that's just a little better every time."

Australian fiction writer D.C. Green agrees. "Finally, you think your book is ready. It isn't. Time to let the manuscript breathe for a month, before revising it with fresh eyes. Be ruthless. Hack those excess adjectives that editors loathe. Delete every scene that does not sparkle, advance the plot on multiple levels and compel the reader to keep reading."

Accepting Criticism

A major challenge for any author is to accept honest criticism of their work. For some writers it is very difficult to separate themselves from their writing and consequently they regard any criticism of it as a criticism of themselves as a person. However, you must, at all times, maintain your objectivity, listen to the comments of others and seriously consider them. Some people are more diplomatic than others but when faced with a forthright comment it is in your interest as the author to listen to it and, if appropriate, ask the person to expand on their opinion. This applies particularly to people involved in the publishing business. After all, their comments are made with the intention of helping you to improve the quality of your writing and ultimately the marketability of your novel.

In the case of *Robyn* I was a male author writing a young adult novel in which the main protagonist was a young woman, as were many of the other characters. My wife is Head of Drama at a large girls' college in Auckland. I gave her my first completed draft, with my name deleted and asked her to give copies to a cross-section of her Year 10 girls, asking them for their written comments.

I was pleased with the generally positive responses, but I carefully read criticisms that referred to the language, and the credibility of some of the incidents. That age group was my target audience and therefore their comments were crucial.

14

IT'S FINISHED: WHAT NOW?

Out of the strains of the Doing

Into the peace of the Done — *Woodruff*

What now? What indeed. The requirements and options are numerous. They include the following key aspects:

The Title of Your Novel

Your novel's title is crucial – in just a few words it should encapsulate the essence of your book.

The title is the first thing that a potential publisher or literary agent will look at. Once your novel is being promoted, the title will appear on all your flyers, posters, websites, interviews and reviews – and, of course, the cover of your novel.

Your title will also be referred to when you are describing it to other people. "My novel is called *Imminent Danger*," or when you're introduced to a group – "Ladies and gentlemen, Mary Jackson, the author of *Imminent Danger*."

The title should be a hook, something that will arouse the reader's curiosity or grab their attention. Include words that are lively, active, descriptive, intriguing – a title that will make the potential buyer pick the book up to find out more.

Check out other titles in libraries and bookstores. Which ones attract you? Why? Consider titles from bestsellers. Are they memorable? *The Day of the Jackal* is one of my favourites, as it immediately conjures up an image of intrigue and menace. *The Spy Who Came in from the Cold*, John Le Carré's first novel, also has a memorable image as do a number of Ian Fleming's novels such as *Goldfinger* or John Connolly's *Every Dead Thing*. Contrasts can be very effective, Jane Austen's *Pride and Prejudice* or Dostoyevsky's *Crime and Punishment* being classic examples. Others can conjure curiosity combined with word pictures, such as New Zealand writer Diane Brown's *Before the Divorce We go to Disneyland*.

Some titles incorporate a subtitle e.g. *Count Me Out: The Chicago Numbers Racket* where the words after the colon offer a brief explanation of the title – probably more common in non-fiction books but worth considering.

Another variation is to have a byline near the title or

somewhere else on the front cover that provides a further clue as to the content – not unlike a movie poster.

Imminent Danger

What do you do when you've run out of options?

You could also consider using a character or spoken line from your novel as the title or as your byline.

Imminent Danger

"So, you've finally run out of options!"

In most cases titles should be short – a maximum of seven words (*Men are from Mars: Women are from Venus* is a notable non-fiction exception).

Often a word or phrase will emerge from your novel's text and provide you with your title or key ideas for the title. You could also try checking your key words in a thesaurus to find synonyms, which may in turn suggest other ideas for your title. A similar idea is to load your keywords into an Internet search engine to see what it produces.

When you finally decide on your title, check it to ensure that there are no other books with the same or similar title. Beware of titles that confuse rather than intrigue, or those with double entendres that may not only confuse but also be offensive to potential readers.

Try your potential title out on friends for their reactions. You'll soon discover whether or not your title appeals, or bemuses, excites or confuses.

My original title was *The Blitzkrieg Boys*. On reflection I decided that the term 'Blitzkrieg' was not widely known to younger adults and could cause confusion among other readers. I then changed it to *Swastika Over the Waitemata*, but decided it was too clumsy. For a while I went with *Raise High the Flag* – based on a translation of the Nazi Horst Wessel Song used in the novel. It embodied action but I finally decided it was too obscure. *Occupation!* followed but was quickly dropped as I felt it wasn't specific enough. I finally decided on *Uncommon Enemy* after reading a newspaper report on a Middle East problem. I liked the ambiguity of the title, an enemy that was uncommon to New Zealand and also an enemy that was not necessarily shared by all the country's occupants – short, thought provoking and easy to remember.

When you start your novel give it a working title to get yourself going and keep it ticking away in the back of your mind. Eventually the right one will come.

The Cover of Your Novel

A cover that immediately attracts the reviewer, retailer or reader is crucial. It is said that 'you can't judge a book by its cover' but nevertheless the cover is the first point of contact with your potential reader. If the cover of your novel does not attract them, they're unlikely to open your flyleaf, let alone read the written pages.

Although the final form of the cover can't be decided until the book is finished and the final proportions and spine size are determined, you should be giving it some thought as your novel takes shape. Browse through bookshops and libraries, studying the covers of novels written for your novel's target readership, considering illustrations, layout, and lettering. Even if you don't consider yourself as having many artistic skills, involve yourself in the process – another part of the pleasure of writing your own novel.

If you have a publisher, work closely with them as they have the experience, and resources, which often include designers. You may in fact prefer to leave the process entirely to them. However, make sure that you have some input, even at the final stage. (When I wrote my first textbook I left the cover entirely in the hands of the publisher's designer and was less than happy with the result.)

For *Uncommon Enemy* I considered a range of options. I finally decided to use a painting of my mother's plus a photograph that I took of a German Luger pistol that I borrowed from a friend. The painting, apart from the personal pleasure of it being my mother's was appropriate inasmuch as it showed a clearly identifiable New Zealand scene while the inclusion of the pistol suggested trouble, violence – reinforced by the book's title *Uncommon Enemy*.

A graphic artist compiled the first draft of the cover. I had it colour printed and laminated on two A3 sheets. One I pinned to my office wall and the other I kept at home. When people dropped in I asked them three basic questions: "If you saw this book cover in a bookseller's Fiction section would you pick it up?" "Why?" " Would you then turn it over to read the blurb on the back?" The basic concept appealed to a range of people but as a result of their comments a few additional modifications were made.

Manuscript Assessors

Manuscript assessors are useful inasmuch as they are professional writers themselves and have knowledge of what constitutes a promising piece of work and its marketing potential. If you are considering the services of a manuscript assessor, ensure that you are clear as to what they will offer – particularly in terms of the assessment of a novel. As always, obtain a clearly stated quote.

I sent my first draft to Graeme Lay, a member of the New Zealand Association of Manuscript Assessors – who review and write reports on manuscripts on a professional basis. I had read the novel a number of times as had others but I wanted an independent, informed opinion before investing any more of my time and energy in it. He charged me a fee to read the novel and write a report on it.

His comprehensive report contained comments that were both encouraging and challenging. The expense was a good investment. I took his advice, re-assessed my plot and characters and began on my second draft.

A Google of 'manuscript assessors' will provide you with plenty of options and a chance to make comparisons in terms of costs and services.

Editors

Some assessors will also offer editing services. Their charges generally range from $20 to $100 per hour. Google 'independent editors' or 'editing services'.

I used an editor for both my novels, and I'm glad I did. She not only picked up some typos but also commented on sentence and paragraph structure, vocabulary, and repetitive use of words. Well worth the investment.

Literary Agents

Literary Agents will represent authors to publishers. In theory they are able to target appropriate publishers and submit your book for consideration by the publisher – on the basis that an endorsement by an agent enhances the chances of being published.

Some agents charge you to read your manuscript before they take you on. Some simply send your book to publishers with a covering letter. Others are more proactive directly contacting targeted personnel within publishing firms. No agent will guarantee publication.

An agent agreed to take me on and submitted my novel to two publishers (a process that took months). After the second submission was turned down, the agent returned my manuscript to me with a brief note. Disappointed, I decided to make my own direct approach to selected publishers.

Letterhead

At this stage someone advised me to design a simple

letterhead. Small printing firms will do this for you, but it's very easy to do on your computer. It's convenient and looks professional when you start corresponding with publishers and others.

Publishers

Remember I said at the beginning that a novel is the hardest form of book to get published, unless you're an author with a track record.

Most publishing houses are prepared to accept manuscripts directly from authors. Guidelines specifying aspects such as layout and typeface are available on request or are featured on their website. Although some will respond quickly, others could take months and then send your novel back without any comment. Don't take it personally – persevere!

Making a Submission

There are many aspiring novel writers like yourself but publishers need to replenish their writing stables, so why not you?

Ensure that your manuscript is clear, clean and error free and matches each of the guidelines specified by the publisher (spacing, font, paper size etc). Surprisingly, publishers continue to receive novel submissions that are of a poor standard in terms of typing, layout, grammar and spelling. So, get ahead of the pack by ensuring that your manuscript is of a high presentation standard.

Find the name of the person responsible for dealing with

unsolicited manuscripts and write a covering letter to them. Include some brief biographical details about yourself.

If you don't want to send the whole novel, you could consider sending extracts accompanied by a synopsis of the plot – on the basis that a publisher might be more inclined to read through this rather than an entire book.

If a publishing house agrees to take your book they will normally bear the cost of printing, marketing and promotion, and you will be paid a percentage of all sales of the book. You will be offered a contract that you should read carefully. If you're uncertain about the contents, take advice. (The New Zealand Society of Authors offers an advisory service regarding contracts and other legal issues to its members.) In the UK the Writers Guild of Great Britain offers contract-vetting services to its members. In the USA The Authors Guild (New York) offers a range of legal services.

Vanity Publishers

Vanity publishers are publishing firms that will print as many copies of your book as you request, for a specified fee. They do not market, promote or sell your book – that's entirely your responsibility. In some cases they offer additional services but, as always, check them out carefully.

Halfway Between

Between the publisher who will pay you a percentage and the vanity publisher who will pay you nothing and offers no services, there are publishing houses that will publish your book for you for a fee but will also offer services such as links with agents, and advice and guidance on the marketing and promotion of your novel. As always, read the small print and obtain a quote.

Self-Publishing

Many authors finally decide to publish their work themselves. One advantage of this process is that you are in full control of all aspects. Inevitably you will need to pay others for some aspects but try to do as much as you can including the word processing, proofreading, layout, and cover design.

The promotional and marketing initiatives can continue for as long as you have the energy and inclination. Typically a commercial publishing house will give your novel three to six months to make an impact on the market. In your case you can maintain the momentum for months, even years. Furthermore, all the profits are yours – instead of only receiving 8% to 10% royalty on the retail price.

You also have the advantage of working to your own schedule, fitting the marketing, promotional activities around your lifestyle and priorities.

As a self-publisher, you will have to consider costs for design, layout, printing and marketing. One rule of thumb: For every dollar of production costs, count on spending at least 20 cents on the marketing and selling of your novel.

All the costs, including marketing are up front – before

you sell your first novel. After that, the marketing costs will continue.

The profits are all yours, but so are the risks. Give it plenty of thought, and carefully question people who offer services that you might need. In other words, do your research before committing yourself.

The costs of layout, proofreading and designing can be fairly high – depending on how much you're able to do yourself. However, I must stress the importance of ensuring that your completed novel is of a high publishing quality. If you're self-publishing, don't skimp on the appearance. Once you've begun the process of marketing and promoting you'll need to have a book that makes a positive impact on the reviewer, the bookseller, the librarian and the retail customer.

Arranging the ISBN Number and Barcode

All books require an ISBN (International Standard Book Number) and barcode. The National Library of New Zealand's website can provide you with an ISBN number and barcode for your novel (www.natlib.govt.nz.) In the USA you have to buy one at $150 or use a service like Smashwords or CreateSpace that provides them free. Nielsen UK ISBN agency provides them at £89.

Legal Deposit

The Legal Deposit requires two copies of all published books to be sent to Legal Deposit Office, PO Box 12340 Wellington.

If you're living outside of New Zealand check on how to obtain an ISBN number, barcode and any legal requirements regarding the depositing of copies of your novel.

Printing Costs

The digital age has considerably reduced printing costs. Printers are now able to offer a POD (Print on Demand) service whereby your book is stored in a computer and comparatively short runs can quickly be made for a standard price. This saves you the risk of printing large numbers of books, having to store them and then worry about selling them to recoup your costs.

Book Distributors and Marketers

If you're fortunate enough to sign a contract with a book publisher, then they will handle your novel's distribution.

If you're going it alone then a book distributor is essential. Using a book distributor's services shouldn't prevent you from promoting and selling the book yourself.

Not all distributors handle fiction. On the other hand, a number of them offer assessment, design, distributing and marketing services. Contact them and discuss their services and costs.

Book distributors are an ever-changing group. The Internet offers a plethora of companies that offer to distribute your novel but, as always, read the small print!

Other Resources

There are also a number of other resources that will help support your dream of writing your first novel.

Books

Elements of Style, Strunk and White, Macmillan 1972 – an excellent book on style, grammar and related areas. Excerpts available on websites.

Not unexpectedly the Internet is full of information for writers. As always you need to troll carefully through its thick shoals. If you have aspirations for publication overseas there are plenty of websites offering to publish your book but *caveat emptor!*

Formatting

The advent of eBooks has opened up a major new option for authors who can now either release their book in print and as an eBook (as I have done) or simply avoid the costs of printing and just have the book available online. I chose both as having a physical copy of my novel, as well as being tangible evidence of my endeavours is also important during my marketing and promotional activities – as well as offering potential buyers a choice.

Websites such as Amazon and Kobo provide instructions for converting your book to an eBook file and uploading it onto appropriate sites. However, I found it easier to leave it to a local publisher. It's not expensive and saves a lot of time and frustration. Consequently, I would recommend going to an eBook-formatting expert.

As well as providing a less expensive means of having your novel available, an eBook is available for an infinite period of time. Books wear out or get lost and the writer or publisher has to then decide whether or not it's worth the trouble and expense of republishing.

eBooks are always there and can be instantly accessed by readers all over the globe. Now there's an incentive for the aspiring authors!

15

SELLING THE
SIZZLE

A novel is a mirror carried along a main road.
— *Stendhal*

Promotion

Even if you are fortunate to be taken on by a royalty-paying publishing house you will still need to be involved in the promotion of your book – don't leave it to the publisher on the basis that they will look after you and your book. Some years ago I had a media textbook published, titled *Media Matters*. It sold out and a second edition was commissioned. It was printed and then I heard nothing further. After extensive enquiries I found that the publishing firm had been taken over and my book had been listed, under the wrong title in the

Romance section of their book listings under the title *Media Mothers*! The moral of the story – keep tabs on your publisher.

If you're investing your own funds then, naturally you'll want to try to sell as many books as possible. Printing the book or putting it on an eBook site is a crucial stage, but your commitment to it has only just begun. Yes, you can feel justifiably proud that you're able to hold your novel in your hand. Now you want as many people as possible to buy it and read it. But they won't buy it if they don't know about it.

Here are a few promotional ideas:

Printed material

Using your cover as a blueprint consider making a poster A3 or A4 that you can take to book readings or place in retail outlets. On a smaller scale, create postcards or business cards that you always have on hand.

Pick Your Time

Try to pick an event, or a date that you can link with the release of your book. If the media is running stories about the event then they're more likely to be interested in a press release from you.

A Book Launch

This is your first chance to create hype and interest in your book. Here are a few ideas:

Invite everyone you can possibly think of – including anyone with whom you've done business or spent money. Use all means of communication – traditional and social media.

Invite local celebrities including MPs, the mayor and councillors. If appropriate, include heads of school, polytechnic or university English departments.

Include booksellers, librarians and the local media. (Don't forget clubs or groups who could be interested in the subject. They are potential buyers and could also invite you as a speaker to their meetings/functions.)

Try to have a story run in your local paper featuring you and your book (think of a local angle) with details of the book launch.

Select a pleasant venue – hall or small theatre.

Ask family and friends to help with the catering. Have some drinks and nibbles.

Play music (live is a good option).

Select someone lively to act as your MC.

Set up a table by the door with copies of your book on display with the price clearly marked.

Have at least two people at the table selling the book. If possible have credit card facilities available or offer the option of direct crediting to your bank account.

Offer a discount, as you're selling direct.

Offer a further discount for three or more copies – on the

basis that your novel will make an excellent Christmas or birthday gift.

Offer to sign all copies – ask the purchaser's name (or the person who will receive the book as a gift) and include a short message addressed to them.

Book Readings

Contact the Head Librarian at your local libraries. Offer to do a reading of your book. Most libraries are keen to help local authors and will host readings and in some cases assist with publicity. Ask them what other authors have done in terms of promotional materials – flyers, brochures, and items in newsletters – in order to maximize your publicity. Also think of an angle (setting, time, characters) that will appeal to local readers. Have copies of your book for sale.

Booksellers

Contact local booksellers – particularly if your book has strong local interest. They may be prepared to feature or display your book or to arrange a link between them and the local library. Be prepared to be flexible, as each bookseller will have different needs.

It's also worth trying secondary schools, tertiary institutions by contacting their librarian – or if you're cheeky enough, send them a copy of your book with an invoice.

Media Publicity

You'll need to give away copies of your novel to book reviewers, and radio and TV hosts. Build this into your expenses.

Prepare a press release for local newspapers or appropriate magazines. Consider linking it with your book launch or library/bookshop reading. Be flexible, as you may want to adapt it for different local areas. Include a high quality photograph of yourself and your book cover.

Contact magazines whose readers might be interested in your novel. Write a general press release that you can alter to fit the type of magazine and its readers.

Contact radio and TV stations – offer to do an interview. Send a list of suggested questions they could ask you about yourself and the areas that the book covers – the more thought-provoking the better.

Advertising

Adverts cost money, so give careful thought to any media that you're thinking of using. Consider the advertorial concept whereby a local paper runs a press release about you and your novel and you in turn take out an advertisement.

If you're using social media to promote your book, consider paying for a banner that will be targeted to your potential readers. Check each of the social media sites for details of cost and processes.

Direct Contact

Print flyers, postcards and direct mail or email targeted groups or people.

Have the flyers or postcards at hand to give to people you meet. Yes, while you should avoid being branded as an insurance salesperson, I've found that most people are interested in meeting someone who has written a novel and are willing to accept a card or to even order a copy. You could also enquire whether they belong to a group that would be interested in having you as a guest speaker. Use your own instinct on each occasion but if the opportunity presents itself, make use of it.

Sales Commission

If your book would make a good gift, see if you can sign up 10–12 students, friends, associates to offer the books to friends and family for 40% sales commission.

Book Clubs

There are book clubs all over the country – often meeting in private homes. Some are listed with local councils. Others are through word of mouth. Track them down and offer to attend a meeting to talk about your book. Ask them what aspect of your novel and your writing would be of particular interest to their members and tailor your talk accordingly. Take copies of your novels along and offer a discount to their members.

Special Interest Groups

Consider groups who might be interested in your novel because of the setting or content.

Service Groups

Service groups, such as Lions, Rotary, Probus are often looking for guest speakers. Contact them and discuss the emphasis you could give to your presentation, and that you would like the opportunity to sell your book.

Charitable Groups

Consider linking with a well-known and relevant non-profit organisation and offer to share the profits ($1.00 per book) for every book they sell to their members. If they have special events, be present and set up a spot where you will sell your book. There are many worthy causes so select one that appeals to you, is well known, has a large membership and a regular publication that would feature you and your book.

Discounts and Added Value

If you're giving a talk to a particular group, offer them a discount price for your novel. "The normal retail is $27.50, but tonight I'm able to offer it for $20.00." ($20.00 is a nice round figure for which there is a monetary note/bill.)

Everybody likes a freebie. You could also consider offering something that would go with your book. (John Connolly, the thriller writer, offers a CD of songs that had inspired him in the writing of his novels.) You might even be able to find a business colleague to sponsor your book, the book launch, or to provide a giveaway with each of your books.

Other giveaways could be bookmarks, postcards, posters (printed at the same time as your cover is printed) or t-shirts. Some of these could be given away in a competition related to your book.

Website

If you have a publisher then your book will be listed on their website. If not, check out the costs of setting up and maintaining your own website. Many authors have one with details of their book and, all importantly, how the book can be purchased. Check out other authors' websites and decide on the features that you'd like in yours. (Mine is drjohnreynolds.com).

Suggestions could include:

- Details of the author and background
- Cover of the book
- Background to the book – photos of location(s), historical event(s) etc
- Reviews/comments
- News of activities related to your book e.g. launches
- Selected excerpts from chapters (don't give the ending away!)
- Recording of readings from the book – your voice or a friend with a suitable voice
- Links to other websites and/or search engines so that your book title will appear during searches

Social Media

The advent of social media (Twitter, LinkedIn, Facebook etc) offers a myriad of opportunities for you to raise awareness and market your novel. For example, even while you're writing it you could post excerpts and ask for comment or provide regular updates on your writing progress. This will build up networks on which you can capitalize at your book launch and subsequent promotional activities. The social media options are constantly changing and expanding. Keep up to date with any new innovations and decide whether or not you can use them to continue to market your novel.

Costs and Expenses

Writing a novel, as well as consuming your time, also consumes your money and resources. If you're writing it to sell, then the process can be deemed to be a business venture with tax-deductible expenses (including a percentage of your rent/mortgage for office space, phone, consumables, travel, accommodation). Check this out with your local taxation office and/or an accountant. Keep all records of expenses (receipts etc) to enable you to make a legitimate claim. Be honest and upfront. Tax allowances will assist you greatly – if you make a loss it will ease the financial burden, if you make a profit you'll have to pay tax, but that's a measure of your success!

16

CONCLUSION

A book is the only immortality. — *Rufus Choate*

Your first novel is unlikely to make you rich. If you break even on costs you can be pleased with yourself. However, if money were your only motivation you'd probably be better off taking an additional part-time job that pays a decent hourly rate.

But, if you've written and published your first novel, held it in your hand, and sold several hundred copies, that's an achievement of which you can be justly proud. You've created your story, you've invented and developed your characters and you've played a godlike role in deciding the paths that their lives took and the fate that awaited them. Nothing and no one can take that away from you.

Yes, there are thousands of people who have written novels, but there are millions who haven't. You may never write another one, but the fact that you have provides you with the potential to further your writing career – as a novelist or in other areas.

Writing a novel takes you on a challenging journey of discovery. At the end is the reward of your very own novel – not to mention the opportunity to enjoy the benefits of celebrity status for a while.

I wish you every possible success!

BIBLIOGRAPHY

Books

Diane Brown, *Before the Divorce we go to Disneyland*, North Shore, Tandem, 1997

Diane Brown, *If the Tongue Fits*, Auckland, North Shore, Tandem, 1999

John Connolly, *Every Dead Thing*, Hodder and Stoughton, London, 1999

Joy Cowley, *Classical Music*, Auckland, Penguin, 1999

Liza Dalby, *Geisha*, Vintage, Random House, London, 2000

Jonathan Delaware, *The Clinic*, Little, Brown and Company, London, 1996

Stevan Eldreg-Gigg, *Oracles and Miracles*, Auckland, Penguin, 1999

John Fowles, *The French Lieutenant's Woman*, Jonathan Cape, London, 1969

Kevin Ireland, *The Man Who Never Lived*, Auckland, Vintage, 1997

Douglas Kennedy, *The Pursuit of Happiness*, Hutchison, London, 2001

D.H. Lawrence, *Lady Chatterly's Lover*, London, Penguin Books, 1960

D.H. Lawrence, *The Rainbow*, Penguin Books, London, 1915

John A. Lee, *The Politician*, Auckland, Century Hutchinson, 1987

John le Carré, *The Pigeon Tunnel*, Penguin Books, London 2016

Iris Murdoch, *Jackson's Dilemma*, London, Penguin, 1995

Iris Murdoch, *The Good Apprentice*, London, Penguin, 1985

Joan Rosier-Jones, *So You Want to Write*, Auckland, Random House, 2004

Vikram Seth, *An Equal Music*, Phoenix, London, 1999

Maurice Shadbolt, *House of Strife*, Auckland, Hodder and Stoughton, 1993

C.K. Stead, *Smith's Dream*, Auckland, New House Publishers, 1996

Philip Temple, *To Each His Own*, Christchurch, Hazard, 1999

Films

Sleeping Dogs, (1977) director: Roger Donaldson

ACKNOWLEDGEMENTS

Writing this book has been a pleasure. It's the teacher in me that enjoys passing on ideas and information to others to help them realise their hopes, dreams and aspirations. The book began as a few thoughts that I put together after completing *Uncommon Enemy*, with the idea of perhaps including them in a pamphlet or booklet to accompany the novel. However the concept rapidly expanded to include a much wider variety of information and examples. In the process of writing my second novel *Robyn Hood Outlaw Princess* (based on one of my full-length musicals) I acquired some additional ideas that I've incorporated into this second edition.

A special thanks goes to my wife Bess, my muse and my most vigorous critic, who encouraged me while at the same time keeping me focussed. Thanks also to my long-time friend John Paton who spent many years in the publishing business and whose comments on my draft manuscript encouraged me in further developing it.

THE AUTHOR

John Reynolds was born in
Auckland, New Zealand. He is
a qualified teacher and has
lived and worked in many
parts of the world, including
England, Saskatchewan
Canada, Zimbabwe, USA and
Australia.

After completing a BA in
History at the University of Auckland, he completed an
MA at San Jose State University, California (with the
assistance of a Creative New Zealand grant), and a PhD at
the University of Auckland in Film, TV and Media
Studies.

As well as being a freelance author, scriptwriter and
broadcaster on radio and TV, he has lectured on media
studies, screenwriting, fiction and academic writing and
related areas, at a number of tertiary institutions.

He is always interested in feedback on his work, and
invites readers to contact him by email
(jbess@vodafone.co.nz) or through his website:
drjohnreynolds.com.

BY THE SAME AUTHOR

Publications

Uncommon Enemy – available on: itunes.apple.com, Amazon.com, barnesandnoble.com, and kobo.com

Robyn Hood Outlaw Princess – available on: itunes.apple.com, Amazon.com, barnesandnoble.com, and kobo.com

Musicals

Robyn Hood Outlaw Princess (Music: Gary Daverne)

Starblaze (Music: Shade Smith)

Windust (Music Shade Smith

Valley of the Voodons (Music Shade Smith)

All musicals available through Stagescripts (www.stagescripts.com) or direct from the author: contact him at jbess@vodafone.co.nz.